Anger Management for Teens Mad to Calm

Holistic approaches, Practical exercises, and Valuable Insights to help Overcome Challenges, Manage Anger, and Build Emotional Resilience

I0458296

By
Agnes Blake

Table of Contents

Introduction

Why Your Emotions Matter and How This Book Can Help

Have you ever felt like your anger gets the best of you? Maybe it's when your blood starts boiling because your friend didn't text back or a sibling borrowed something without asking. It's as if a storm suddenly erupts inside, and you're left wondering how to calm it down. If that sounds familiar, you're not alone.

I remember being a teen and feeling like my emotions were a rollercoaster I couldn't control. One day, I was on top of the world, and the next, I was angry at everything—from schoolwork to friends. There was one time when I lost my cool at a soccer game. I was so frustrated with my performance that I yelled at my teammates. Looking back, I wish I had known then what I know now about managing anger and emotions.

This book is here to help you navigate those stormy emotions with practical tools and techniques. It's designed to give you the skills to manage anger, improve emotional intelligence, and build healthier relationships. We'll explore ways to turn anger into something positive, using it as a stepping stone for growth rather than a stumbling block.

The book is structured to guide you step-by-step. We'll start by understanding what anger is and why we feel it. Then, we'll explore techniques to calm down at the moment and dig deeper into the roots of our frustrations. From there, we'll tackle the pressures teens face today, like social media stress and peer relationships. Each chapter builds on the latter, creating a roadmap to emotional balance and self-awareness.

This journey will benefit you as a teen and be a valuable resource for parents. Parents will gain insights into supporting their child's emotional growth and learn strategies to strengthen family bonds. Together, families can work towards creating an environment where everyone feels understood and respected.

Let's face it—being a teen today isn't easy. There are academic pressures, the constant buzz of social media, and the challenge of fitting in with peers. These stresses can build up, and sometimes anger is the only way to express them. Acknowledging these challenges is the first step in managing them.

By the end of this book, you can expect to feel more in control of your emotions. You'll gain self-awareness, learn how to communicate effectively and find a greater sense of emotional balance. These skills will not only help you now but will also set a strong foundation for the future.

I invite you to embark on this journey of transformation. The exercises, reflections, and stories you'll find here are not just words on a page. They're tools for change, meant to be engaged with and reflected upon. This book is more than a guide—it's a partner in your journey toward personal growth and family harmony.

So, let's get started. Together, we'll turn anger from a force that divides into a force that unites and empowers. Grab your pen and journal for an unforgettable journey!

Chapter 1: Understanding Anger and Its Roots

Discover the "Why" Behind Your Reactions and What Fuels the Fire

Have you ever wondered why a seemingly minor comment from a friend could send you into a spiral of irritation or why a minor mishap can feel like the end of the world? Anger can be puzzling, especially when it seems to erupt out of nowhere. It's like having an unpredictable storm brewing inside, catching you off guard. As a teen, I often felt like I was constantly battling these unexpected tempests, unsure of why they happened or how to calm them. Understanding the roots of anger is the first step toward managing it, and that journey begins in the brain, where tiny, unseen processes significantly impact how we feel and respond.

The Science of Anger: What Happens in Your Brain

When you experience anger, your brain is complicated at work, processing emotions in complex ways. At the heart of this process is the amygdala, a small, almond-shaped cluster of nuclei deep within the brain. The amygdala acts like an emotional alarm system. It's quick to react to perceived threats or stressors, signaling something is wrong, which can trigger an immediate emotional response. This is what often leads to intense feelings of anger. But the amygdala doesn't work alone. The prefrontal cortex, located at the front of the brain, plays a crucial role in regulating these emotions. It helps you analyze situations, consider consequences, and make rational decisions. However, the amygdala can override the prefrontal cortex during intense anger, leading to impulsive reactions without much thought. This is particularly true during adolescence when the brain is still developing, and the prefrontal cortex is not yet fully matured (SOURCE 1).

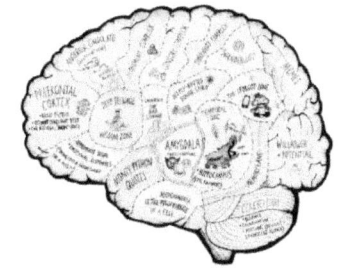

Hormones like adrenaline and cortisol also affect how you experience anger. Adrenaline, often called the "fight or flight" hormone, prepares your body to react to threats by increasing your heart rate and energy levels. Cortisol, the stress hormone, helps your body manage long-term stress. Together, these hormones can heighten emotional states, making anger more intense and immediate. Adolescents are susceptible to these hormonal changes, exacerbating emotional responses (SOURCE 1).

Beyond these immediate reactions, the concept of neuroplasticity offers hope. Neuroplasticity is the brain's ability to reorganize itself by forming new neural connections. Your brain can change and adapt based on your experiences and practices. By consistently applying anger management techniques, you can train your brain to respond differently, enhancing emotional control over time. This adaptability is key in transforming how you perceive and react to frustrating situations, allowing you to respond more calmly and thoughtfully.

Understanding these biological processes can empower you to manage your emotions more effectively. Knowing why your body reacts in a certain way makes it easier to take control. You can start recognizing the signs of an emotional response before it spirals, allowing you to engage your prefrontal cortex and make conscious choices about reacting. This knowledge turns anger from a mysterious and overpowering force into something you can manage and use to your advantage. Recognizing these brain mechanisms helps demystify anger, allowing you to approach it with curiosity and understanding rather than fear or frustration.

Source 1

Dynamic mapping of human cortical development

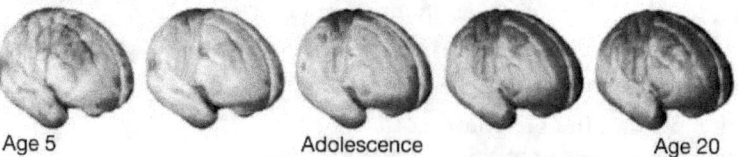

Age 5   Adolescence   Age 20

Source: "Dynamic mapping of human cortical development during childhood through early adulthood," Nitin Gogtay et al., Proceedings of the National Academy of Sciences, May 25, 2004; California Institute of Technology.

Interactive Element: Stress and Anger Checklist

Take a moment to reflect on situations that typically trigger your anger. Grab a notebook and write down these triggers. Next to each, note how your body and mind respond. Do you feel your heart racing? Does your mind start racing with thoughts? This exercise helps you recognize patterns in your emotional responses, providing insight into your brain's workings. Understanding these patterns is the first step in changing them, giving you more control over your reactions and helping you to approach situations with a calmer mindset.

Stress and Anger Checklist

Take a moment to reflect on your emotions and responses. Use the prompts below to guide your journaling. Write your answers directly on the lines provided.

Step 1: Identify Your Triggers

What situations or events typically make you feel angry or stressed?

Example: Being stuck in traffic, feeling misunderstood, or being criticized.

Write your triggers below:

_____

_____

_____

_____

Step 2: Observe Your Physical Reactions

How does your body respond in these moments?

Example: Heart racing, muscle tension, or stomach discomfort.

Write your physical reactions below:

_____

_____

_____

_____

Step 3: Track Your Mental Reactions

What happens in your mind when you feel angry or stressed?

Example: Racing thoughts, jumping to conclusions, or feeling overwhelmed.

Write your mental reactions below:

_____

_____

_____

_____

Step 4: Reflect on the Patterns

Look at your responses above. Do you notice any patterns in how you react?

Example: I often clench my fists when angry or assume the worst in stressful situations.

Write your observations below:

_____

_____

_____

_____

Step 5: Commit to Change

How can you use this awareness to respond differently in the future?

Example: Practice deep breathing, count to ten, or take a moment to step away.

Write your action plan below:

_____

_____

_____

_____

This journaling exercise helps you become more mindful of your emotional patterns, paving the way for positive change!

Hormonal Hurricanes: Navigating Teenage Changes

The teenage years are a whirlwind of change, and much of it is driven by hormones. Puberty is like a storm that sweeps through, changing not just your body but also your emotions and how you see the world. It's no wonder that anger can sometimes feel like a constant companion during this time. Hormones like testosterone and estrogen take the stage during these years, each uniquely shaping emotional experiences. For many boys, increased levels of testosterone can lead to heightened aggression and irritability. While essential for growth and development, this hormone often amplifies feelings of competitiveness and frustration.

Meanwhile, girls experience fluctuations in estrogen, which can lead to mood swings that sometimes feel out of control. These hormonal changes aren't biological but deeply intertwined with how we perceive and react to the world.

These hormonal shifts impact boys and girls differently. Boys might feel a surge of energy and impatience, leading to outbursts over things that seem trivial later. On the other hand, girls might find themselves riding an emotional rollercoaster, where one moment, they're elated, and the next, they're in tears. Understanding these differences can be enlightening, not just for teens but for parents, too. It highlights the need for empathy and patience, as these changes are part of growing up. The way these hormones influence emotions can sometimes make it feel like they're running the show, but there are ways to regain control.

Managing these hormonal impacts involves a combination of healthy habits and open communication. Diet plays a crucial role in stabilizing mood. Eating balanced meals with whole grains, lean

FEELINGS AND EMOTIONS

Identifying feelings and emotions is crucial because it helps understand ourselves, communicate effectively with others, and build strong, empathetic relationships

CHEERFUL · EXCITED · SATISFIED

HAPPY · PROUD · LOVED

PLAYFUL · CALM · SICK

EMBARRASSED · SURPRISED · SHY

SLEEPY · SAD · ANGRY

TIRED · WORRIED · HURT

DISAPPOINTED · CONFUSED · SCARED

proteins, and plenty of fruits and vegetables can help maintain energy levels and emotional stability. Regular exercise is another powerful tool. Physical activity releases endorphins, the body's natural mood lifters, which can counteract feelings of anger and frustration. Sleep, often overlooked, is vital. A good night's rest can significantly influence how you handle stress and emotions the next day. When well-rested, you're more likely to think clearly and react calmly.

Open dialogue about these changes is key. Talking about what you're going through with someone you trust—a parent, teacher, or friend—can be incredibly freeing. It's important to remember that you're not alone in this. Everyone goes through it, and having a support system can make a difference. Expressing how these hormonal changes affect you can help those around you understand your behavior better. It can also lead to finding solutions together, whether adjusting your routine or finding new ways to cope with overwhelming feelings.

Interactive Element: Hormonal Journal Prompts

Find hormones confusing? To help you navigate these changes, try keeping a journal. Here are a few prompts to get you started: "Describe a day when you felt overly angry or emotional. What triggered those feelings?" "Reflect on the times you felt calm and in control. What were you doing differently?" Writing about your  experiences can help you identify patterns and find strategies that work for you. This practice enables you to understand yourself better and provides a space to vent and process your emotions safely. Use the worksheet below:

Worksheet: Hormonal Journal Prompts

Understanding and Managing Your Emotions

Keeping a journal is a great way to explore your emotions, identify triggers, and discover what works for you in managing your feelings. Use the following prompts to reflect on your experiences and better understand your emotional responses.

Part 1: Reflecting on Emotional Responses

1. **Describe a day when you felt overly angry or emotional.**

   o   What happened that day?

   o   What triggered your feelings?

   o   How did you react to those emotions?

   (Write your response here.)

   _____

   _____

   _____

2. **Reflect on the times you felt calm and in control.**

   o   What was different about those moments?

   o   What were you doing to stay calm and balanced?

   o   How did it feel to have control over your emotions?

(Write your response here.)

_____

_____

_____

_____

Part 2: Identifying Patterns

After completing the above reflections, review your answers and consider the following questions:

- Do you notice any common triggers for your intense emotions?

- Are there activities, environments, or people that help you feel calm and in control?

- What changes can you make to your daily routine to effectively manage your emotions?

(Write your response here.)

_____

_____

_____

_____

Part 3: Setting Goals and Strategies

Based on your reflections:

1. **What is one thing you can do differently next time you feel overwhelmed?** *(Write your goal here.)*

_____

2. **What can you do to create more calm moments?** *(Write your strategy here.)*

_____

_____

Tips for Successful Journaling

- Write honestly and without judgment—this journal is for you.

- Try to journal regularly, even if it's just for a few minutes a day.

- Use this space to vent, brainstorm, and explore solutions to help you grow.

By taking the time to write and reflect, you're investing in your personal growth and well-being. Keep practicing, and you'll find strategies that work best over time!

Family Dynamics: The Role of Home Environment

Family can be a source of comfort and support and a pressure cooker of emotions and expectations. How a family interacts can significantly influence a teen's emotional state, often tipping the scales toward either peace or turmoil. For instance, parents' guidance and discipline can make a big difference. An authoritative style, which balances firm guidance with warmth and open communication, can help teens feel secure and understood. In contrast, an authoritarian approach—strict, with little room for dialogue—may leave teens feeling trapped and rebellious, leading to more frequent outbursts of anger. It's like being in a classroom where the teacher only shouts orders without explaining why; eventually, frustration bubbles over.

HAVING FAMILY * TIME IS * IMPORTANT

Spending time with your family can increase happiness and satisfaction

WHY DO WE NEED TO SPEND TIME WITH OUR FAMILY?

Spending quality time with your family can encourage open communication and help establish loving relationships.

OTHER BENEFITS OF SPENDING TIME WITH FAMILY

• Strengthen family bonds
• Promotes adaptability and resilience
• Fulfills emotional needs
• Boosts Self-Confidence

Sibling rivalry adds another layer of complexity to family dynamics. Competition for attention or resources can stoke the fires of resentment and anger. Imagine constantly feeling like you're in a race with your sibling, vying for the limited spotlight in a busy household. This competitive environment can significantly exacerbate feelings of inadequacy and frustration if one sibling consistently outshines the other. These dynamics can create a cycle of rivalry and anger, making home life more like a battlefield than a haven.

External stressors also play a significant role in shaping the emotional climate at home. Financial stress can be a silent yet powerful force, casting a long shadow over family interactions. When money is tight, tensions can rise, and everyone feels the ripple effects. Teens might pick up on the stress, leading to feelings of anxiety and anger that aren't always easy to articulate. Similarly, parental conflict—

frequent arguments or a tense silence—can leave a teen feeling caught in the middle, unsure how to navigate the emotional minefield. These stressors can amplify emotional responses, making it harder for teens to regulate anger.

Creating a supportive home environment starts with open communication. It's about building a space where everyone feels heard and valued. This means having regular family check-ins, where members can express what's on their minds without fear of judgment. It's like opening a window in a stuffy room, letting fresh air and light in. This practice helps identify and address issues before they escalate and strengthens family bonds. Parents and teens can work together to create family rules or agreements, fostering a sense of shared responsibility and respect.

Encouraging honest conversations about feelings and challenges can transform a household. It's essential to approach these talks with empathy and patience, understanding that everyone is working through their struggles. For example, a teen might not always know how to articulate their anger, but with gentle guidance, they can learn to communicate more effectively. This might involve using "I" statements, such as "I feel upset when..." instead of placing blame. Parents can model this behavior, showing teens how to express emotions constructively and calmly, turning potential conflicts into opportunities for growth.

Like in any group, family dynamics can shift and change over time. Acknowledging this fluidity and being willing to adapt is key. By fostering a nurturing and communicative environment, families can create a foundation where teens feel supported in navigating their emotions. This support can act as a buffer against adolescence's external pressures and internal changes, offering teens a stable base to face the world.

Past Experiences: Unpacking Childhood Influences

The past has a funny way of sticking with us, sometimes in ways we don't even realize. Early experiences linger beneath the surface for many teenagers, quietly shaping reactions and feelings. It's like when a song from childhood suddenly plays, and you're flooded with memories—some good, some not so much. Past traumas or significant events can leave marks on our emotional skin, influencing how we respond to the world around us. Whether it's a memory of  being bullied in elementary school or the ache of a parent's divorce, these experiences can affect the way you handle anger today. Childhood trauma, in particular, can be like carrying a heavy backpack you forgot you were wearing. It affects your posture, your movements, and sometimes, your mood. The weight of those early experiences can manifest as quick tempers or unexplained sadness, even years later.

Beyond specific events, early attachment styles play a critical role in how emotions unfold during the teenage years. Attachment theory suggests that how you bond with caregivers as a child influences your relationships and emotional responses as you grow. For instance, a secure attachment tends to foster confidence and resilience. However, if the attachment is anxious or avoidant, it might lead to feelings of insecurity or difficulty trusting others. Imagine building a house on shaky ground; it might stand for a while, but the foundation could give way under stress. Recognizing these influences can be the first step toward understanding why certain situations trigger intense emotions.

Recognizing signs of unresolved past issues isn't always straightforward. It might be as simple as noticing patterns—like reacting disproportionately to criticism or feeling overwhelmed in specific situations. For a teen, this could mean realizing that every time a teacher raises their voice, it reminds them of past scoldings, triggering a defensive response. Parents, too, might notice that their teen withdraws after family arguments, a sign that echoes past experiences. These behaviors can be clues pointing to the past, asking for attention and understanding.

Addressing these lingering effects involves more than just acknowledgment. It requires actively working through them, often with help. Therapy and counseling are potent tools for unpacking these emotions and learning new coping methods. A therapist can offer a safe space to explore these feelings, providing  strategies to heal and move forward. They act as guides, helping you navigate the complex landscape of your emotions. Journaling can also be incredibly therapeutic. You create a dialogue with yourself by writing down thoughts and feelings, uncovering hidden emotions and patterns. It's like holding up a mirror to your mind, reflecting on what you see without judgment.

Resilience and growth aren't just buzzwords but tangible outcomes from facing past challenges. There are countless stories of individuals who have overcome difficult childhoods to build fulfilling lives. These stories inspire and remind us that the past doesn't have to define the future. Take, for example, someone who grew up in a tumultuous household yet learned to channel their experiences into a passion for helping others. Their past became a source of strength and empathy rather than a chain holding them back. This transformation is possible for anyone willing to face their history with courage and openness.

Building resilience means embracing the lessons of the past while forging a new path forward. It's about accepting that while you can't change what happened, you can change how it affects you. This process takes time, patience, and, often, a bit of help. But it's a journey worth taking, leading to a deeper understanding of yourself and a more peaceful relationship with your emotions. Embracing this growth can help turn past challenges into stepping stones, rather than stumbling blocks, on the path to emotional health.

Peer Pressure: Fitting In vs. Standing Out

Peer pressure is an invisible force that can feel overwhelming, especially during the teenage years when fitting in seems vital. Imagine being in a school cafeteria where everyone's wearing the latest sneakers, and you're stuck in last year's kicks. It's not just about shoes; it's about wanting to belong. This pressure to  conform can lead to frustration and anger, particularly when it clashes with personal values. It's as if you're wearing a mask to fit in, suppressing your true self to avoid standing out for fear of exclusion. This fear can become a powerful motivator, pushing teens to act against their nature to remain in the group.

The constant need to compare oneself with others adds another layer to this struggle. Social comparison is like a double-edged sword. On one hand, it's natural to look around and see what others are doing. On the other hand, it can exacerbate feelings of inadequacy and anger. When everyone else seems to have it all together or looks perfect, it's easy to feel like you don't measure up. This can lead to anger directed inward, as you berate yourself for not being enough, or outward, as you lash out at others for seemingly having it more manageable. It's a cycle that can be hard to break, feeding on insecurity and self-doubt.

So, how do you resist the negative pull of peer pressure while staying true to yourself? It begins with assertiveness, a skill that allows you to stand firm in your beliefs without alienating others. Think of assertiveness as saying, "This is who I am, and I'm okay with it." It's about setting boundaries and expressing your needs clearly, even when it feels intimidating. Building a supportive network of friends who respect and encourage your individuality can make a significant difference. These friends celebrate your quirks and support your choices, providing a safe space to be yourself without fear of judgment.

Authenticity is your most incredible tool. Embracing what makes you unique is not just empowering; it's liberating. When you stop trying to fit into a mold that doesn't suit you, you can channel your energy into pursuits that genuinely bring you joy and fulfillment. Whether it's a passion for painting, a love for science fiction, or an interest in environmental activism, these are the things that define you. They are the colors that paint your canvas, making you stand out in the best possible way.

The value of being authentic cannot be overstated. It builds self-confidence and creates a ripple effect, inspiring others to do the same. It's like being a beacon in the fog, showing others that it's okay to be different. When you embrace your true self, you attract the right people into your life—the ones who appreciate you for who you are, not who you're pretending to be. This authenticity creates genuine connections and deepens existing relationships, allowing you to form bonds based on mutual respect and understanding.

Navigating peer pressure is challenging but also an opportunity to learn more about who you are and what you stand for. Each time you choose to be yourself, you strengthen your character and resilience despite the pressure to conform. It's a step toward self-discovery and personal growth, replacing anger and frustration with confidence and peace.

Digital Distress: The Impact of Social Media

Picture this: you wake up, and the first thing you do is grab your phone. Notifications flood the screen, drawing you into a world of endless scrolling. Social media is everywhere, and while it connects us, it also brings a unique set of challenges. Imagine the constant connectivity like a buzzing background noise that never lets you relax. It's no wonder that this digital world can lead to increased anxiety and anger. The pressure to stay connected and the fear of missing out can create a cycle of stress that's hard to break. Social media platforms, while offering a sense of community, often become arenas for comparison and competition. Every post, like, or comment adds pressure to maintain a perfect online persona. It's like curating an art gallery where each piece must be flawless, leaving no room for vulnerability or imperfection. This pressure can lead to feelings of inadequacy and frustration, as the desire to project a particular image overshadows the reality of who you are.

Cyberbullying is another dark side of this digital space. It's an issue that can't be ignored. The internet's anonymity can embolden individuals to say things they'd never dare to utter face-to-face. Hurtful comments and messages can have a profound emotional toll, leaving scars that aren't visible but are deeply felt. It's the modern-day equivalent of whispers behind your back, but they can only reach you anytime, anywhere. This can lead to feelings of isolation and anger as victims struggle with the constant barrage of negativity.

The effects of digital interactions on self-esteem are significant. Social media often sets an unrealistic standard for beauty, success, and happiness. It's easy to fall into the trap of measuring your worth by the number of likes or comments. This digital validation becomes a double-edged sword, providing temporary gratification and fueling a more  profound sense of inadequacy when the likes don't match expectations. It's like chasing a moving target, always out of reach, leaving a trail of frustration and self-doubt.

To combat this digital distress, adopting healthy digital habits is crucial. Think of it like setting boundaries in any other relationship. Scheduled digital detox periods can provide much-needed breaks from the constant influx of information. Unplugging for a few hours each day or dedicating a day a week to being offline allows your mind and emotions to rest and reset, much like a mini-vacation for your brain. Mindful social media usage is another powerful tool. This means being intentional about how and when you engage online. Consider curating your feed to include content that inspires and uplifts rather than comparing or critiquing.

Promoting a positive digital presence is about using social media as a platform for good. Focus on sharing content that reflects your true self, interests, and passions. Whether posting about a hobby, sharing a personal achievement, or simply connecting with others over shared interests, use your online presence to express who you are authentically. It's about shifting from a place of performance to a genuine connection. By doing this, you improve your experience and contribute to a more supportive and positive online community.

In this hyper-connected world, finding a balance between online and offline life is key. It's not about cutting out social media entirely but using it to enhance rather than detract from your life. By setting boundaries and focusing on authentic connections, you can navigate the digital landscape with confidence and calm. This approach reduces digital stress and strengthens your mental and emotional well-being, allowing you to engage with the world—both online and offline—in a healthier, more balanced way.

Chapter 2: Developing Emotional Intelligence

Know Yourself, Name Your Emotions, and Take Back Control

Imagine being in a heated argument, where your heart races and your mind is a whirlwind of thoughts. We've all been there, feeling that rush of emotions and not knowing how to handle it. Emotional intelligence is about understanding these feelings and learning to manage them effectively. It's like having a toolbox for your emotions, where each tool helps you handle different situations more skillfully. Developing this intelligence is not just about feeling better but thriving in your relationships and personal life.

Recognizing emotional triggers is crucial and often the first step toward emotional control. Triggers are those little things that trigger an emotional reaction, sometimes so quickly that you barely notice them until you're upset. It could be unfair treatment in a group project at school, where one person doesn't pull their weight, leaving you to pick up the slack. Or perhaps it's the pressure of an upcoming exam, with expectations bearing down on you like a heavyweight. These situations can provoke anger, and understanding why they affect you so deeply is key to managing your reactions.

To identify these triggers, start by reflecting on your past experiences. Keep an emotional diary—it's a simple yet powerful tool. Write down moments when you felt angry, noting what happened, who was involved, and how it made you think. Over time, patterns will emerge. You may notice that certain situations consistently provoke a strong response. Maybe it's when you're in crowded places or when plans change unexpectedly. These insights are invaluable because they help you predict and prepare for similar situations in the future.

Once you've identified your triggers, the next step is to anticipate them. This doesn't mean avoiding life but equipping yourself with strategies to handle challenging scenarios. Visualization is a practical technique. Picture a situation that might provoke you, like a competitive sports match or a group discussion. Imagine how you might feel and visualize  yourself handling it calmly and confidently. This mental rehearsal prepares your mind, making you more likely to respond with poise when the situation arises.

Developing proactive responses is about planning constructive ways to deal with known triggers. Think of it as creating a personal action plan. For example, if public speaking makes you anxious, you should practice deep breathing before and during the event. Or if you know a particular friend's teasing tends to upset you, decide in advance to address it directly and calmly. Having these strategies ready is like having a map in unfamiliar territory—it guides you and helps prevent emotional outbursts.

Interactive Element: Trigger Reflection Exercise

Take a moment to jot down a few situations that often spark anger. Next to each, write how you typically react and consider how you might respond differently. This exercise isn't about judging your past reactions but exploring new possibilities and preparing for future encounters.

Building emotional intelligence is an ongoing process. It's about learning to navigate life's ups and downs with greater ease and understanding. Recognizing triggers and preparing for them, you develop resilience and self-awareness, paving the way for healthier relationships and a more balanced life. Whether you're a teen facing the daily challenges of school or a parent navigating family dynamics, these skills are invaluable. They empower you to take control of your emotional landscape and respond to life's challenges confidently and calmly.

Anger Reflection Journal

Date: [Insert Date] _____

Part1: Identifying Situations That Spark Anger

Take a moment to reflect on recent
situations that have triggered anger.
Write down a few examples describing
the context and the emotions you felt.

1. **Situation:** [Brief description of the event]

_____

_____

_____

_____

_____

_____

o   **How I Typically React:** [Describe your usual response]

_____

_____

_____

_____

- **How I Could Respond Differently:**
  [Write a potential new approach]

_____

_____

_____

_____

2. **Situation:** [Brief description of the event]

_____

_____

_____

_____

- **How I Typically React:** [Describe your usual response]

_____

_____

_____

_____

o **How I Could Respond Differently:**
[Write a potential new approach]

_____

_____

_____

_____

3. **Situation:** [Brief description of the event}

_____

_____

_____

_____

o **How I Typically React:** [Describe your usual response]

_____

_____

_____

_____

o **How I Could Respond Differently:** [Write a potential new approach]

_____

_____

_____

_____

Part 2: Reflecting on Patterns and Possibilities

Answer the following questions to deepen your understanding:

1. **What common themes or triggers do I notice in these situations?** [Write your response here]

_____

_____

_____

_____

2. **How do my typical reactions affect my relationships and personal well-being?** [Write your response here]

_____

_____

_____

_____

3. **What tools or strategies could help me respond more calmly and constructively?** [Write your response here]

_____

_____

_____

_____

4. **How can I remind myself to use these new approaches in the moment?** [Write your response here]

_____

_____

_____

_____

Part 3: Building Emotional Intelligence Reflect on the importance of emotional growth and resilience in managing anger.

1. **What have I learned about myself through this exercise?** [Write your response here]

_____

_____

_____

_____

2. **How can recognizing and preparing for triggers help me navigate challenges more effectively?** [Write your response here]

_____

_____

_____

_____

3. **What steps can I take to continue developing emotional intelligence?** [Write your response here]

_____

_____

_____

_____

Part 4: Moving Forward Summarize your insights and identify one specific action you can take to practice a healthier response to anger.

- **Summary:** [Write your summary here]

_____

_____

_____

_____

- **Actionable Step:** [Write one small, specific step you'll take]

_____

_____

_____

_____

This journal is a space for self-exploration and growth. Revisiting it regularly can help you stay attuned to your progress and remain committed to building resilience, self-awareness, and healthier relationships.

Self-Awareness Exercises: Know Thyself

Have you ever wondered why certain events stir up strong emotions while others barely make a ripple? Self-awareness is like a spotlight that illuminates these hidden corners of your mind, offering clarity and understanding. Developing this awareness starts with self-reflection, a practice that invites you to look  closely at your thoughts and feelings. Each day, set aside a few moments to ask yourself questions like, "What emotions did I experience today?" or "How did I react to challenges?" This daily reflection helps you connect the dots between your experiences and emotions, revealing patterns you might not have noticed before. It's like piecing together a puzzle, where each answer brings a new level of understanding.

Another powerful tool for self-discovery is personality assessments, like the Myers-Briggs Type Indicator (MBTI). This assessment helps you explore your emotional tendencies, highlighting your natural preferences and how they shape your interactions with the world. For instance, you might discover that you're more introverted, finding energy in solitude, or perhaps you're an extrovert, thriving in social settings. Understanding these traits can clarify why you react differently in different situations. Analyzing your personality profile is like looking at a map; it shows where you are now and offers insight into how you navigate life. While the MBTI is not the definitive word on who you are, it provides a framework for exploring your strengths and areas for growth.

Once you have a clearer picture of your personality, you can move on to identifying your core values—those guiding principles that influence your decisions and emotional responses. Imagine these values as the compass that directs your actions and choices. They might include honesty, compassion, or creativity. Spend some time reflecting on what matters most to you and why. This could be a values identification workshop, where you list things that resonate deeply with you. Knowing your values is like having a personal guidebook; it helps you understand why certain situations evoke strong emotions and ensures your actions align with your beliefs.

Promoting self-compassion is equally crucial, especially when emotions are running high. Being kind to yourself means recognizing that everyone struggles and makes mistakes—including you. Instead of harsh self-criticism, practice speaking to yourself as you would to a friend, with understanding and patience. When you catch yourself in a critical thought loop, pause and ask, "Would I say this to someone I care about?" This shift in perspective can transform your inner dialogue, fostering a nurturing environment where growth and healing can occur. It's about permitting yourself to be human, to experience a range of emotions without judgment.

Interactive Element: Personal Values Reflection

To explore your core values, try this exercise. Write down ten qualities or principles that feel important to you. Then, narrow the list to five, focusing on the most resonating. Reflect on how these values influence your daily life and decisions. This practice clarifies what drives you and strengthens your sense of self, providing a solid foundation for emotional intelligence.

These self-awareness exercises are more than just activities; they're pathways to understanding yourself better. By engaging in self-reflection, personality assessments, and values exploration, you create a rich tapestry of insights that guide you through life's emotional landscape. Coupled with self-compassion, these practices empower you to embrace your unique identity and navigate challenges gracefully and confidently. As you deepen your self-awareness, you unlock new potential for emotional growth, transforming how you relate to yourself and others.

Personal Values Reflection Journal

Date: _____

Part 1: Identifying My Core Values

Take a moment to brainstorm and list ten qualities or principles you hold dear. These could be traits, beliefs, or ideas that define who you are or guide your actions.

1. _____

_____

2. _____

_____

3. _____

_____

4. _____

_____

5. _____

_____

6. _____

_____

7. _____

_____

8. _____

_____

9. _____

_____

10. _____

     _____

Part 2: Narrowing Down to My Top Five Values

Review the list above and reflect on which values resonate with you
most deeply. Select the five values most essential to your identity and
life decisions.

1. _____

    _____

2. _____

    _____

3. _____

    _____

4. _____

    _____

5. _____

    _____

Part 3: Reflecting on My Values

Answer the following questions to deepen your understanding of how these values influence your life:

1. **Why do these five values stand out to me?**

   [Write your response here]

   _____

   _____

2. **How do these values influence my daily choices and actions?**

   [Write your response here]

   _____

   _____

3. **How do these values guide me during challenging times?**

   [Write your response here]

   _____

   _____

4. **What can I do to further embody these values in my life?**

   [Write your response here]

   _____

   _____

Part 4: Moving Forward

Summarize your reflections and identify one actionable step to strengthen your alignment with your core values.

- **Summary:**

  _____

  _____

  _____

  _____

- **Actionable Step:**

  [Write one specific step you'll take]

  _____

  _____

Emotional Vocabulary: Naming Your Feelings

Imagine trying to describe a painting using only a handful of colors. You might capture the basic outlines, but the nuances, depth, and emotion would be lost. Emotions are a lot like that. When we limit ourselves to basic terms like "happy" or "angry," we miss the richness of our emotional experiences. There's a whole spectrum of feelings, each with its subtle shade. Expanding your emotional vocabulary can help you articulate what you're genuinely feeling. Instead of just "angry," you might feel "frustrated" when things don't go your way or "disappointed" when someone lets you down. Words like "overwhelmed" capture the sense of everything being too much, while "content" describes a quiet satisfaction. Having the right words is like having the right tools—they make it easier to express yourself accurately and understand others.

Practicing emotion identification in various contexts is a great way to get familiar with these words. Consider a recent social scenario: maybe you were at lunch with friends, and someone made a joke that rubbed you the wrong way. What did you feel? Was it "irritation" or "embarrassment"? By role-playing different situations, you can practice identifying and naming these emotions as they arise. It could be as simple as acting out a family disagreement or a classroom debate. The goal is to pause and label each feeling, noticing how it shifts as the situation unfolds. This practice enhances your emotional vocabulary and boosts your emotional intelligence, making it easier to navigate the ups and downs of daily life.

Precise language is crucial for emotional regulation and communication. When you can accurately name your feelings, you take ownership of those emotions. It turns a vague, unsettling sense of unease into something tangible you can address. For instance, telling someone, "I'm feeling overlooked," is much more effective than simply expressing anger. It opens the door for constructive dialogue and solutions. Precise language also helps in self-reflection, allowing you to pinpoint the cause of your feelings and address them head-on. It's like having a map for your emotions, guiding you through the maze of your inner world with clarity and purpose.

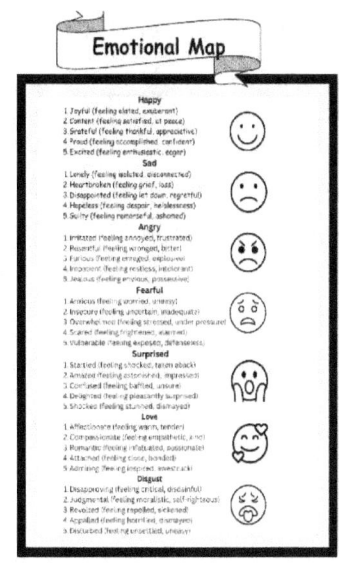

Creating emotion charts or maps can be a helpful visual tool in this process. Picture a chart divided into sections labeled with different emotions and their variations. You might have a section for "anger," branching into "frustration," "rage," and "annoyance." Another for "sadness" could include "melancholy," "grief," and "disappointment." Having this visual reference can aid in quickly identifying your emotional state, especially when words seem elusive. It can also serve as a reminder of the complexity of emotions, validating that it's okay to feel multiple things at once. This chart becomes a personal resource, a go-to guide for understanding and managing emotions in real time.

Interactive Element: Create Your Emotion Map

Grab some paper or use a digital tool to create your emotion map. Start with broad categories like "happy," "sad," and "angry," then branch out into more specific emotions like "joyful," "lonely," and "irritated." As you go through your day, refer to this map, marking the emotions you experience. Reflect on how accurately you can name your feelings and how this awareness impacts your interactions. This exercise deepens your understanding of emotions and encourages empathy as you become more attuned to the emotional experiences of others around you.

Building a rich emotional vocabulary is like adding more colors to your palette. It allows you to paint a fuller picture of your experiences for yourself and others. Practicing this skill enhances your ability to communicate effectively and connect with others. Emotional vocabulary is a powerful tool in your emotional intelligence arsenal, fostering more profound understanding and healthier relationships.

Daily Emotion Tracker Form (use the Emotional Map above)

Date: _____

---

1. Track Your Emotions

- **Emotion**   **Experienced:**

_____

- **Time:**

_____

- **Recurring?** [ ] Yes [ ] No (Use additional rows if needed)

- **Emotion**   **Experienced:**

_____

- **Time:**

_____

- **Recurring?** [ ] Yes [ ] No

---

2. Reflect on Your Emotions

For each emotion you tracked, reflect on the following:

- **Emotion:** _____

  o What triggered this emotion?

  _____

  o How did I react?

  _____

  o Could I have reacted differently?

  _____

(Repeat for additional emotions as needed)

_____

3. End-of-Day Review

- Did naming my emotions help me regulate them better?
  [ ] Yes   [ ] No Notes:

  _____

- How did my awareness of emotions affect my interactions with others?

Notes:

  _____

Journaling for Clarity: Writing Your Emotions

Imagine your mind as a cluttered desk. Thoughts and feelings are scattered everywhere, and it's hard to find what you need when everything's in a jumble. Journaling is like organizing that desk, putting each piece of paper in its place so you can think clearly. There are countless ways to journal, and finding the right style can make all the difference. Stream-of-consciousness journaling might be your go-to if you prefer to let your thoughts flow freely. This involves writing whatever comes to mind without worrying about grammar or structure. It's like conversing with yourself, where you can vent, ponder, and explore without judgment. On the other hand, bullet journaling offers a more structured approach, using concise bullet points to capture key thoughts and events. It's a practical way to keep track of emotions and patterns over time. Some prefer prompt-based journaling, where specific questions guide their reflections. Prompts like "What emotion did I feel most strongly today and why?" can open doors to deeper insights, helping you explore emotions you might not even realize you have.

Regular journaling has a host of benefits. It's about recording your day and gaining clarity and understanding. Writing about your emotions helps you process them, breaking down complex feelings into manageable parts. It's like untangling a knot, slowly working through each twist and turn until you can see the whole picture. This practice can also highlight triggers and patterns in your responses, allowing you to approach future situations more clearly. Over time, you'll notice how journaling offers relief as if you're unloading a heavy weight from your shoulders. It provides a safe space to express thoughts and feelings that might be difficult to share with others.

To make journaling a regular habit, having a few prompts ready is helpful. These can serve as starting points, sparking introspection and guiding your writing. Consider questions like "What made me smile today?" or "How did I handle a challenging situation?" These prompts encourage you to reflect on positive and negative experiences, providing a balanced perspective. Another powerful practice is keeping a gratitude journal. In it, jot down things you're thankful for each day. They don't have to be big—sometimes, small moments bring the most joy, like a kind word from a friend or a beautiful sunset. This can shift your focus from what's wrong to what's right, fostering a more positive outlook.

Interactive Element: Daily Gratitude Prompt

Set aside time each evening to write down three things you're grateful for. Reflect on why these moments stood out and how they made you feel. Over time, this practice can help you see the good in your daily life, even when things seem harsh.

Journaling is a profoundly personal journey, and there's no right or wrong way to do it. The key is to find a style that resonates with you and make it part of your routine. Whether you journal every day or a few times a week, putting pen to paper (or fingers to keyboard) can be transformative. It offers a window into your inner world, helping you better understand yourself and navigate life's challenges more confidently and calmly. As you continue to explore your emotions through journaling, you'll uncover layers of insight and self-awareness that enrich your life unexpectedly.

How to Use This Worksheet

1. **Set Aside Time:** Choose a consistent time each evening for journaling practice.

2. **Create a Calm Environment:** Find a quiet space without distractions.

3. **Be Honest:** Write from the heart. There's no right or wrong way to journal.

4. **Reflect:** Consider why each moment stood out and how it made you feel.

Daily Gratitude Prompts

Day 1:

1. What are three things you're grateful for today?

_____

_____

2. Why did these moments stand out?

_____

3. How did these moments make you feel?

_____

Day 2:

1. Think about someone who made your day better. What did they do?

_____

_____

2. What simple pleasure brought you joy today?

_____

_____

3. Describe a moment of peace or calm you experienced.

_____

_____

_____

_____

Day 3:

1. Reflect on a personal accomplishment, no matter how small.

_____

_____

2. What natural beauty did you notice today?

_____

3. Who or what inspired you today?

_____

Repeat similar prompts for 30 days to build a consistent gratitude habit.

Reflect and Grow

Weekly Reflection:

1. Looking back over the week, what patterns do you notice in your gratitude entries?

   _____

   _____

2. How has your perspective shifted?

   _____

   _____

3. What moments of gratitude surprised you?

   _____

   _____

Monthly Reflection:

1. How has your emotional well-being changed since you started this practice?

   _____

   _____

_____

_____

2. What new insights have you gained about yourself?

_____

_____

3. How can you continue to incorporate gratitude into your daily life?

_____

_____

Section 5: Tips for Long-Term Success

- **Be Consistent:** Even on tough days, find one small thing to be grateful for.

- **Mix It Up:** Use different prompts to keep your practice fresh.

- **Celebrate Progress:** Acknowledge the effort you've put into your journaling.

- **Share Your Gratitude:** Expressing your appreciation to others deepens your practice.

Conclusion

Journaling is a profoundly personal journey that offers insight and self-awareness. As you continue this practice, remember to be kind to yourself and embrace the transformative power of gratitude. Over time, you'll uncover the beauty and joy even in life's smallest moments.

Mindfulness and Meditation: Finding Your Center

In the hustle and bustle of everyday life, finding a sense of calm can feel like chasing a mirage. Mindfulness offers a way to see through the chaos and find clarity. It's about tuning into the present moment and noticing what's happening around you without getting swept away. One of the simplest ways to start practicing mindfulness is through guided breathing exercises. By focusing on the rhythm of your breath, you anchor yourself in the present, quieting the noise of the mind. Imagine sitting comfortably, eyes closed, taking slow, deep breaths. Inhale, feel the air fill your lungs, then exhale, releasing tension with each breath. This practice is like hitting the reset button, giving you space to pause and regroup.

Another technique to ground yourself is the body scan meditation. During this practice, you bring awareness to different body parts, starting from your toes and working your way up to the top of your head. It's about noticing sensations, whether the tension in your shoulders or the warmth in your hands, without judgment. As you focus on each area, you release any tightness or stress, feeling your body relax with each exhale. This meditation enhances body awareness and fosters a sense of connection and presence. It's a gentle reminder that you're here now, and that's enough.

Exploring meditation techniques can further deepen your emotional well-being. Loving-kindness meditation, for example, is a practice that cultivates compassion and empathy. It involves silently repeating phrases that express good wishes for yourself and others. You might think, "May I be happy, may I be healthy, may I live with ease," then extend these wishes to friends, family, and even those you find challenging. This practice nurtures feelings of warmth and kindness, softening the edges of anger and frustration. It's like planting seeds of positivity, which grow into a garden of understanding and acceptance.

Regular mindfulness and meditation practice offers numerous benefits, from reducing stress to improving emotional regulation. When you consistently engage in these practices, you develop a greater capacity to handle life's ups and downs calmly and clearly. It's like strengthening a muscle; the more you practice, the more resilient you become. Over time, you'll notice a shift in how you respond to challenges. Instead of reacting impulsively, you pause, assess, and choose a thoughtful response. This change doesn't happen overnight, but with patience and commitment, it becomes a natural part of your life.

Creating a personal meditation space can enhance your practice. This doesn't have to be elaborate—a cozy corner with a cushion, a soft blanket, a candle, or plants. The key is to create an environment that feels inviting and peaceful, a place where you can retreat and recharge. Having a dedicated space signals to your mind that it's time to slow down and focus inward. It's a sanctuary from the world's busyness, a space to connect with yourself and find your center.

Emotional Intelligence in Action: Real-Life Scenarios

Emotional intelligence often comes to life in the stories of everyday people who learn to navigate their emotions with skill and empathy. Take, for instance, the story of Jake. Jake was a typical teen juggling schoolwork, extracurriculars, and a social life. But there was one area where he struggled—peer conflict. In his friend group, disagreements often escalated into full-blown arguments, hurting and misunderstanding everyone. One day, after another argument over a group project, Jake decided to try something different. Instead of reacting defensively, he paused and listened. He asked his friends how they felt and shared his own feelings calmly. This shift in approach transformed the conversation. Instead of pointing fingers, they worked together to find a solution that satisfied everyone. Jake's ability to manage his emotions and communicate effectively strengthened his friendships, showing how emotional intelligence can turn conflict into collaboration.

Practicing emotional intelligence doesn't have to be limited to real-life situations. Role-playing scenarios can be an invaluable tool for honing these skills. Imagine a simulated family disagreement, where each person plays a role, much like actors in a play. In this safe setting, you can experiment with different responses, trying out strategies that might feel risky in real life. Maybe you practice expressing your feelings clearly or work on listening without interruption. Each role-play is a rehearsal for real-life interactions, where you can test out emotional intelligence techniques and see what works best for you. It's a chance to learn and grow without the pressure of real-world consequences.

The impact of emotional intelligence on relationships is profound. When you approach interactions with empathy and understanding, you create a space where true connection can flourish. Think about how much easier it is to open up to someone who listens without judgment or supports you without trying to fix your problems. This is the essence of emotional intelligence—building bridges of trust and communication that strengthen bonds. In families, this might mean parents and teens working together to navigate the challenges of adolescence with mutual respect. It might involve offering support during tough times or celebrating successes without jealousy among friends. These skills enhance relationships, making them more resilient and fulfilling.

After practicing these scenarios, it's crucial to reflect on the experience. Take a moment to evaluate your performance, identifying what went well and where there might be room for improvement. Ask yourself questions like, "How did I handle my emotions?" or "What could I have done differently?" This reflection helps solidify your learning, making each practice a stepping stone for future growth.

Consider seeking feedback from others in the role-play, as their perspectives can offer valuable insights. This continuous cycle of practice, feedback, and reflection is how emotional intelligence becomes second nature, evolving from a set of skills into an integral part of who you are.

Interactive Element: Reflection and Feedback Session

Gather a group of friends or family members and choose a scenario to role-play. Afterward, discuss what you noticed about your reactions and communication. Share feedback, focusing on strengths and areas for growth. This exercise builds emotional intelligence and strengthens your support network, creating a community where everyone is committed to growth and understanding.

As you apply emotional intelligence in everyday life, you begin to see its transformative power. It's about managing emotions and using them to connect, empathize, and communicate more effectively. These skills are the foundation for more prosperous, meaningful relationships with friends, family, or yourself. With each practice, you build a toolkit that equips you to handle life's challenges with grace and confidence. Emotional intelligence is a journey without a final destination, constantly evolving and expanding as you learn.

Reflection and Feedback Session Worksheet

Interactive Element: Role-Playing for Emotional Intelligence

Date of Session:

_____

Facilitator (if applicable):

_____

Scenario Chosen for Role-Play:

_____

_____

Participant Reflection

1. What emotions did you experience during the role-play?

_____

_____

2. How did you express these emotions? (e.g., tone, body language, words)

_____

_____

3. Did you notice any moments where your emotions influenced your communication style? If so, how?

_____

_____

4. What were the biggest challenges for you during the scenario?

_____

_____

5. What strengths did you demonstrate in your reactions or communication?

_____

_____

6. What areas for improvement did you notice in your reactions or communication?

_____

_____

_____

Group Feedback

1. What did the group observe about your emotional and communication strengths?

_____

_____

2. What constructive feedback or suggestions did the group offer for improvement?

_____

_____

3. Did you notice any recurring themes across feedback given to multiple participants? (e.g., empathy, listening, tone)

_____

_____

_____

Takeaways for Growth

1. What specific skills or strategies would you like to practice or develop further?

_____

_____

2. How can your support network help you strengthen these skills?

_____

_____

3. What steps will you take to apply emotional intelligence in everyday life?

_____

_____

_____

Participant Signatures

(Optional, to signify commitment to growth and mutual support)

Name: _____

Signature: _____

Name: _____

Signature: _____

Name:_ _____

Signature: _____

Chapter 3: Practical Strategies for Managing Anger

Tools and Techniques to Stay Cool When Life Heats Up

Imagine you're in the middle of a heated argument. Words are flying, emotions are high, and you can feel your heart pounding like a drum in your chest. It's a familiar scene for many, but wouldn't it be incredible to have a tool that helps you find calm amid the chaos? That's where breathing techniques come in. They might seem simple, but these exercises are powerful. They can quickly transform a tense moment into one of clarity and control. It's like having a reset button for your emotions, allowing you to pause and choose how to respond.

Breathing Techniques: Instant Calm for Intense Moments

The science of deep breathing is fascinating because it directly taps into your body's natural systems to create calm. When you take controlled, deep breaths, you activate the parasympathetic nervous system. This part of your nervous system is responsible for rest and digestion, counteracting the fight-or-flight response that kicks in during stressful moments. By calming the body, you also calm the mind, making it easier to think clearly and make thoughtful decisions. One particular method, diaphragmatic breathing, focuses on breathing deeply into your belly rather than shallowly into your chest. This technique allows more oxygen to enter your bloodstream, lowering heart rate and decreasing stress.

Let's dive into some specific breathing exercises you can use. Box breathing is a simple yet effective method. Picture a square as you breathe. Inhale through your nose for a count of four, hold your breath for another four, exhale slowly through your mouth for four, and pause for four counts before starting again. It's like drawing a box with your breath; each side brings you closer to calmness. Another popular technique is the 4-7-8 method. Start by

59

inhaling quietly through your nose for four seconds. Hold the breath for a count of seven and then exhale completely through your mouth for eight seconds. This extended exhale helps release tension and stress, leaving you feeling more relaxed and grounded.

The benefits of breath control are immediate and profound. These techniques can instantly reduce stress and anger in a heated moment. Imagine a stormy sea suddenly calming to a gentle ripple; that's what controlled breathing can do for your emotions. Focusing on your breath creates a mental space to step back from the chaos, allowing you to assess the situation with a clearer mind. It's like having an internal anchor keeping you steady when everything else feels overwhelming.

Regular practice of these exercises can build a habit of calmness over time. Incorporating them into your daily routine can enhance their effectiveness, like regular exercise strengthens muscles. Start small—maybe with a few minutes each morning or evening—and gradually increase as you become more comfortable. You might find it helpful to pair these exercises with a routine activity, like brushing your teeth or waiting for the bus. Over time, you'll notice that your ability to manage stress and anger improves, leading to a more balanced and peaceful life.

Interactive Element: Daily Breathing Practice Checklist

Use the checklist below to track your breathing practice. Make time for morning and evening sessions, with space to note how you felt before and after each practice. Reflect on any changes in your stress levels or emotional responses throughout the day. This checklist can help reinforce the habit and make it easier to see the benefits of regular practice.

Breathing techniques offer a simple yet powerful way to manage anger and stress. By understanding and practicing these methods, you equip yourself with tools to navigate emotional challenges more effectively. They provide a pathway to calmness and clarity, transforming how you experience and respond to the world.

Techniques used for breathing.

Diaphragmatic Breathing

Also known as belly breathing, this technique focuses on deep, slow breaths that engage the diaphragm rather than shallow chest breathing.

How to practice:

1. Sit or lie down in a comfortable position.

2. Place one hand on your chest and the other on your stomach.

3. Inhale deeply through your nose, ensuring your stomach rises while your chest stays still.

4. Exhale slowly through your mouth, feeling your stomach fall.

5. Repeat for a few minutes, focusing on the rhythmic movement of your breath.

Box Breathing

This structured breathing technique involves inhaling, holding, exhaling, and holding your breath for equal counts, forming a "box" pattern.

How to practice:

1. Inhale through your nose for a count of 4.

2. Hold your breath for a count of 4.

3. Exhale slowly through your mouth for a count of 4.

4. Hold your breath again for a count of 4.

5. Repeat the cycle for a few minutes.

Alternate Nostril Breathing

In yoga, this technique is known as Nadi Shodhana. It involves breathing alternately through each nostril to balance energy and calm the mind.

How to practice:

1. Sit in a comfortable position with a straight spine.

2. Use your thumb to close your right nostril and inhale deeply through your left nostril.

3. Close your left nostril with your ring finger and release your thumb to exhale through your right nostril.

4. Inhale through the right nostril, close it with your thumb and exhale through the left nostril.

5. Repeat this cycle for several minutes, focusing on smooth and even breaths

Daily Breathing Practice Checklist

Morning Session

1. **Date:** _____

2. **Start Time:** _____

3. **Duration (minutes):** _____

4. **Technique Used:**

   o   ☐ Diaphragmatic Breathing

   o   ☐ Box Breathing

   o   ☐ Alternate Nostril Breathing

   o   ☐ Other: _____

5. **How I Felt Before Practice:**

   o   ☐ Calm

   o   ☐ Stressed

   o   ☐ Angry

   o   ☐ Anxious

   o   ☐ Other: _____

6. **How I Felt After Practice:**

   o   ☐ Calm

   o   ☐ Relaxed

   o   ☐ Focused

   o   ☐ Still Stressed (but less intense)

o ☐ Other: _____

Evening Session

1. **Date:** _____

2. **Start Time:** _____

3. **Duration (minutes):** _____

4. **Technique Used:**

   o ☐ Diaphragmatic Breathing

   o ☐ Box Breathing

   o ☐ Alternate Nostril Breathing

   o ☐ Other: _____

5. **How I Felt Before Practice:**

   o ☐ Calm

   o ☐ Stressed

   o ☐ Angry

   o ☐ Anxious

   o ☐ Other: _____

6. **How I Felt After Practice:**

   o ☐ Calm

   o ☐ Relaxed

   o ☐ Focused

o ☐ Still Stressed (but less intense)

o ☐ Other: _____

Reflection Section

1. **Notable Changes in Stress/Emotional Levels Throughout the Day:**

---

2. **Did Breathing Practice Help Me Navigate Emotional Challenges Today?**

   o ☐ Yes, definitely

   o ☐ Somewhat

   o ☐ Not really (Why?): _____

3. **Insights or Thoughts for Improvement:**

By reviewing this checklist regularly, you can track patterns in your emotional well-being and observe how consistent breathing practice transforms your ability to handle stress and anger.

Physical Outlets: Channeling Anger into Activity

There's something almost magical about how physical activity can transform a bad mood. When you're angry or stressed, your body is flooded with adrenaline, urging you to fight or flee. Exercise taps into this natural response, channeling that energy into something productive. It's like turning a raging river into a powerhouse that generates strength and calmness. Endorphins, the body's natural feel-good chemicals, are released during physical activity. These little wonders help reduce stress hormones, making you feel more relaxed and positive. Moving your body can be a powerful antidote to anger, whether it's a brisk run around the park or an intense martial arts session.

Running or jogging is one of the most accessible forms of exercise, requiring nothing more than a pair of good shoes and a little motivation. The rhythmic nature of running provides a meditative experience, allowing your mind to untangle thoughts while your feet pound the pavement. Each step can feel like shedding a layer of frustration, replaced by a sense of accomplishment. Similarly, martial arts offer a structured way to channel aggression. The discipline and focus required in martial arts improve physical fitness and teach valuable lessons in patience and self-control. It's a space where you can release pent-up energy in a supportive environment, leaving you feeling centered and empowered. Dance or movement classes are another fantastic outlet. Expressing emotions through movement can be liberating, turning negative energy into a creative force. Whether hip-hop, ballet, or contemporary dance, moving to music can be a joyful way to let go of anger.

Consistent exercise is key to reaping long-term emotional benefits. Making physical activity a regular part of your life builds resilience against stress and anger. It's like strengthening a muscle—the more you use it, the stronger it becomes. Regular exercise enhances physical health and sharpens mental clarity, making it easier to handle life's challenges. The discipline of sticking to an exercise routine can spill over into other areas of life, fostering a sense of accomplishment and control. Encouraging teens to explore different physical activities can open up new avenues for self-expression and well-being. Trying various sports or exercises allows you to find what resonates best with your interests and needs. It might be team sports like soccer or basketball, which offer camaraderie and a shared goal, or solo activities like yoga or swimming, which provide a more introspective experience. The important thing is to enjoy the discovery process, knowing that each new activity is a chance to learn about yourself.

Interactive Element: Physical Activity Exploration Chart

The chart below lists various physical activities you might want to try or add your own. It includes columns for your initial impressions, any challenges you face, and how you felt afterward. This chart is a personal record of your exploration, helping you identify which activities best help you manage anger and stress.

Finding the right physical outlets is not just about staying fit; it's about creating a toolkit for emotional well-being. Each activity adds a layer of resilience, helping you navigate life's ups and downs more easily. As you experiment with different forms of exercise, you'll improve your physical health and discover new aspects of yourself, fostering a deeper connection to your body and emotions. This self-discovery is rewarding, offering a sense of empowerment and confidence beyond the gym or playing field.

Samples of Activities to try:

1. Pilates

2. Tennis

3. Rowing

4. Trail Running

5. CrossFit

6. Archery

7. Paddleboarding

8. Ice Skating

9. Soccer

10. Surfing

11. Add your own

Physical Activities	Initial Impressions	Challenges	How You Felt After

Creative Expressions: Art as an Emotional Outlet

Sometimes, words just aren't enough to express what you're feeling. That's where art comes in. Artistic expression offers a unique way to process and release emotions that might be too tangled or intense to articulate. Picture this: you're sitting with a blank canvas, a palette of colors before you, and a world of emotions inside. As you dip your brush and paint, each stroke becomes a pathway for your feelings to travel. Whether angry, sad, or joyful, painting or drawing can help you externalize those feelings, turning chaos into something tangible and beautiful. Creating can be meditative, allowing you to lose yourself in the moment and find clarity and calm. It's about translating those inner storms into something outside of yourself so they don't feel overwhelmed.

The beauty of creative expression lies in its diversity. If painting isn't your thing, perhaps writing poetry or stories is. Words have a rhythm and flow that can capture emotions in a powerful and healing way. You might find solace in crafting a poem that captures the essence of your feelings or in writing a story where you can control the narrative and outcomes. It's a way to reclaim your voice and assert control over unwanted emotions. Playing a musical instrument offers another avenue for expression. Music has an incredible ability to convey feelings without saying a word. Whether you're strumming a guitar, playing the piano, or beating a drum, each note can echo the emotions you're experiencing, providing a release that words sometimes cannot achieve. These forms of self-expression allow you to explore different facets of your emotional world, offering insight and release.

Starting a creative project might seem daunting, especially if you don't consider yourself an "artist." But remember, art isn't about perfection; it's about expression. Begin with simple steps, like doodling in the margins of your notebook or writing a few lines of verse. Gradually, as you become more comfortable, you can expand your skills and explore new mediums. Take a class, join a club, or set aside weekly time to create. The key is to allow yourself the freedom to experiment and make mistakes. Art is a personal journey, and each piece you create is a step toward understanding yourself better.

Inspiration can be found in countless stories of individuals who have creatively transformed their emotions. Take, for example, a young woman who turned to painting during a tumultuous period. Each canvas became a diary of her journey, capturing moments of pain, reflection, and healing. Over time, her artwork helped her process her emotions and became a source of inspiration for others going through similar experiences. Or consider the story of a teenager who found solace in writing music. What began as a way to cope with feelings of isolation grew into a passion that connected him with others and gave him a sense of purpose. These examples show how art can be a powerful tool for healing and connection, turning personal struggles into shared experiences that resonate with others.

Creating art is like opening a window to your soul. It allows you to explore the depths of your emotions and express them in a free and fulfilling way. Whether painting, writing, or making music, these creative outlets offer a refuge from the world's noise, where you can be yourself without judgment or expectation. As you explore these artistic paths, you'll find that the act of creation itself is a journey of discovery, revealing the beauty in the world around you and within.

Digital Detox: Balancing Online and Offline Worlds

It's no secret that screens have become a staple in our daily lives. From smartphones to laptops, we're constantly connected, and while technology has its perks, it can also be a source of stress and anger. Think about it—how often have you found yourself scrolling through social media only to feel a  pang of jealousy or frustration? This phenomenon, often referred to as social media comparison stress, can take a toll on your mental health. When you're bombarded with highlight reels of others' seemingly perfect lives, it's easy to feel inadequate. These emotions can simmer beneath the surface, leading to an increase in stress and even anger. The pressure to keep up with trends and maintain an online persona can be exhausting, leaving little room for genuine self-reflection or relaxation.

To combat the negative effects of constant connectivity, it's important to establish boundaries with technology. One effective strategy is scheduling screen-free times. Consider designating certain day hours, like during meals or before bed, as tech-free zones. This helps reduce screen time and encourages more meaningful interactions with those around you. It's about creating moments of presence where you can fully engage with the world offline. Think of it as allowing your mind to breathe, free from the digital noise. Another practical tip is to turn off non-essential notifications. This simple action can prevent the constant barrage of alerts that pull your attention away from the present moment. By setting clear boundaries, you reclaim control over your time and focus, allowing space for calm and introspection.

Developing offline hobbies is another crucial aspect of achieving balance. Engaging in activities that don't involve screens can provide a refreshing change of pace and help reset your mental state. Imagine going for a hike or a nature walk, where the only notifications you receive are the rustling leaves and chirping birds. The physical act of moving through nature offers a grounding experience, helping you reconnect with yourself and the world around you. Or perhaps you enjoy gardening, cooking, or crafting—activities that require your full attention and offer a sense of accomplishment. These hobbies not only serve as a break from screens but also foster creativity and mindfulness. They remind you of the simple pleasures in life, often overshadowed by the digital hustle.

Mindful technology use is about being intentional with your online interactions. It's not about cutting out technology entirely but rather using it in a way that serves you rather than controls you. Start by curating your social media feeds to include content that inspires and uplifts you. Follow accounts that align with your values and interests, and don't hesitate to unfollow those that trigger negative emotions. It's your digital space, and you have the power to shape it. Another approach is to set specific goals for your online time. Whether it's researching a new hobby, connecting with friends, or learning something new, having a purpose can prevent aimless scrolling and help you make the most of your digital interactions. By practicing mindful technology use, you transform your relationship with screens, making it a tool for empowerment rather than a source of stress.

Finding a balance between the online and offline worlds is an ongoing process. It requires self-awareness and a willingness to make changes that support your well-being. As you experiment with digital detox strategies, you'll discover what works best for you, creating a lifestyle that promotes both mental clarity and emotional resilience. This balance not only enhances your mood but also enriches your daily experiences, allowing you to engage with life more fully and authentically.

Conflict Resolution: Turning Arguments into Discussions

Conflict is a part of life, but how we handle it makes all the difference. When disagreements arise, it's tempting to raise your voice and dig in your heels. But imagine a different outcome, where conflicts become opportunities for understanding rather than battles to win. Key principles of conflict resolution can transform arguments into meaningful discussions. It starts with active listening, which means genuinely hearing what the other person is saying without interrupting or planning your following rebuttal. Listening actively shows that you value the other person's perspective, laying the groundwork for mutual respect. Empathy plays a crucial role, too. Putting yourself in the other person's shoes creates a bridge of understanding that can turn adversaries into allies. And let's not forget compromise; it's about finding a middle ground where both parties feel heard and respected, even if it means giving a little to gain a lot.

A structured approach can help navigate conflict effectively. Begin with "I" statements to express your feelings without casting blame. Instead of saying, "You never listen to me," try, "I feel unheard when I'm interrupted." This subtle shift focuses on your experience rather than accusing the other person, reducing defensiveness. Next, engage in finding common ground exercises. Start by identifying shared goals or values. Maybe you both want a harmonious home environment or a successful group project. Highlighting these commonalities shifts the focus from what divides you to what unites you. It's like focusing on the whole picture rather than getting lost in the details. As you progress, keep the conversation open and honest. It's important to acknowledge each other's points without dismissing them. This validates the person's feelings and opens the door to constructive dialogue.

Respect is the cornerstone of any successful conflict resolution. Maintaining respect during disagreements can prevent escalation and keep the conversation productive. Remember that the person you're arguing with has their own experiences and emotions influencing their perspective. Respect doesn't mean you have to agree, but it does mean acknowledging the other person's right to their view. This approach helps de-escalate tension and fosters an environment where solutions can flourish. If voices start to rise, pause and take a breath. Sometimes, a moment of silence can reset the tone and remind everyone of the ultimate goal: resolution, not victory.

Conflict resolution skills can be applied in various scenarios, from family disagreements to school debates. Imagine a situation at home where chores are a constant source of tension. Instead of letting frustration simmer, gather everyone involved for a discussion. Use active listening to understand each person's viewpoint and work together to find a fair solution. Maybe you establish a rotating schedule or agree on a reward system for completed tasks. In a school setting, when a group project leads to differing opinions, use these skills to facilitate a productive meeting. Encourage each team member to express their ideas, acknowledge strengths and weaknesses, and collaborate to create a plan that leverages everyone's talents. These scenarios illustrate how turning arguments into discussions resolves the immediate issue, strengthens relationships, and builds trust.

Interactive Element: Conflict Resolution Role-Play

Gather friends or family members and choose a common conflict scenario. Assign roles and practice a structured conflict resolution approach, focusing on active listening and empathy. Afterward, discuss what strategies worked well and where there might be room for improvement. This role-playing exercise provides a safe space to  experiment with new skills and gain confidence in handling real-life conflicts.

By embracing conflict resolution principles, you transform potential clashes into opportunities for growth and connection. These skills foster healthier relationships and equip you to navigate life's inevitable challenges with grace and wisdom. Conflict doesn't have to be a barrier; it can be a path to deeper understanding and stronger bonds.

1. **Describe the scenario:** What conflict did your group choose to role-play? Who played which roles, and what was the situation about?

_____

_____

2. Active Listening: How well did the group members listen to each other? What techniques were used to show active listening (e.g., repeating back, asking clarifying questions, or maintaining eye contact)?

_____

_____

_____

_____

3. Empathy in Action: How did each participant demonstrate empathy during the exercise? Did anyone acknowledge feelings or validate perspectives effectively?

_____

_____

_____

_____

4. What worked well? What strategies or approaches helped resolve the discussion? Be specific about what contributed to the success.

_____

_____

_____

_____

5. Challenges and improvements: What parts of the role-play felt difficult or didn't work as well as expected? What could be done differently next time?

_____

_____

_____

_____

6. Personal takeaway: What did you learn about resolving conflicts from this exercise? How can you apply these skills in real-life situations?

_____

_____

_____

_____

_____

_____

Humor and Anger: Laughing it Off

Have you noticed how a good laugh can lighten even the heaviest mood? Humor is a remarkable tool for diffusing anger and tension, offering a fresh perspective on challenging situations. When you are caught in a moment of frustration, a well-timed joke or a funny observation can shift your mindset, easing the intensity of your emotions. It's as if laughter clears the fog, allowing you to see the situation differently. This is because laughter triggers the release of endorphins, those feel-good chemicals that promote a sense of well-being and relaxation. Watching a comedy routine or a funny movie can relieve stress, turning an otherwise tense environment into one that feels more manageable and light-hearted.

Incorporating humor into your daily life can be a healthy way to cope with stress and anger. Consider starting your day with a humorous video or a light-hearted podcast. These moments of joy can set a positive tone for the hours ahead. Sharing jokes with friends or family can reinforce social bonds, creating a shared experience that fosters connection. Even amid a heated discussion, introducing a touch of humor can break the tension and open the door to more constructive dialogue. It's important to remember that humor isn't about making light of serious issues but rather about finding a way to approach them with a bit of levity. When used appropriately, it can transform a conflict into an opportunity for understanding and reconciliation.

However, it's crucial to be mindful of when and how you use humor, as it can sometimes backfire. Jokes that belittle or dismiss someone's feelings can escalate a situation rather than defuse it. Inappropriate humor, especially in sensitive contexts, might come across as insensitive or even hurtful. This is why

timing and context are essential. Using humor as a tool for deflection can also prevent necessary conversations from happening, leaving underlying issues unresolved. It's about striking a balance, knowing when to lighten the mood and when to engage seriously. When handled with care, humor can be a powerful ally in managing emotions and fostering positive interactions.

Countless stories of individuals have effectively used humor to navigate difficult emotions. Take the example of a teacher who noticed their students were agitated during exams. Instead of adding to the stress, they began each session with a funny story or a silly dance. This eased the students' nerves and created a more relaxed and open learning environment. Or consider the story of a parent who used humor to connect with their teenager. During a heated disagreement, they cracked a light joke about the situation's absurdity, and the shared laughter helped bridge the emotional gap. When applied thoughtfully, these anecdotes illustrate how humor can change the emotional landscape, turning potential conflict into moments of connection and understanding.

Humor is invaluable in your emotional toolkit, offering a way to navigate life's challenges with a smile. When you embrace laughter, you invite a sense of relief and perspective that can transform how you handle anger and stress. It's not about avoiding serious issues but about finding a way to approach them that doesn't add to the pressure. As you integrate humor into your life, you'll discover its power to soften hard edges and lighten heavy loads, making each day brighter and more manageable.

As we round off this chapter on practical strategies for managing anger, we've explored various tools—from the grounding power of breathing techniques to the expressive release of creativity and movement. Each plan offers a unique way to channel emotions constructively, equipping you with skills to navigate the complexities of daily life. In the next chapter, we'll delve into building resilience and confidence, crucial elements for sustaining emotional growth and strength.

Chapter 4: Strengthening Relationships

How to Communicate Clearly, Build Trust, and Heal Conflict

Picture yourself in a bustling café, the clatter of cups and the hum of conversation surrounding you. Amid this lively backdrop, you sit across from a friend, eager to share a story that's weighed on you. Your friend's eyes drift to their phone as you speak, nodding absentmindedly at all the wrong moments. Suddenly, you feel like you're speaking to a wall, your words lost in the noise. This scenario highlights a common struggle in our fast-paced world—how often do we truly listen? The art of active listening is a powerful tool that can transform relationships, turning mere exchanges into meaningful connections. When we listen intently, we hear words and the emotions and thoughts behind them, creating a bridge of understanding.

Active listening is more than a technique; it's the cornerstone of healthy communication. It involves paying close attention to verbal and non-verbal cues, ensuring the speaker feels heard and valued. This practice helps reduce misunderstandings and fosters trust, making it an invaluable skill in resolving conflicts. Imagine a heated argument with a sibling or parent, where emotions run high and words are sharp. By employing active listening, you open a pathway for empathy and clarity, shifting the focus from winning an argument to understanding each other's perspectives. It's like diffusing a ticking time bomb with patience and kindness, turning a potential explosion into a calm conversation.

Several techniques can help master active listening. Start with maintaining eye contact, which signals your interest and engagement in the conversation. It's like saying, "I'm here with you," without uttering a single word. Nodding occasionally and using verbal affirmations like "I see" or "Go on" encourages the speaker to continue, knowing they have your full attention. Paraphrasing is another powerful tool. After the speaker finishes, repeat what you've heard in your own words, like a brief summary. This confirms your understanding and gives the speaker a chance to clarify if needed. Reflective listening, where you acknowledge the speaker's emotions, adds another layer. For instance, saying, "It sounds like you're feeling really overwhelmed," shows empathy and validates their feelings.

Body language plays a crucial role in effective listening. It's not just about what you say but how you present yourself. Leaning slightly forward, keeping an open posture, and avoiding distractions like your phone make the speaker feel valued. Non-verbal cues can often speak louder than words, conveying a sense of warmth and sincerity. Imagine a friend pouring their heart out, and you respond with crossed arms and a wandering gaze. Your body language might tell a different story even if your words are supportive. Aligning your verbal and non-verbal signals ensures that your message of support and understanding is loud and clear.

Interactive Element: Active Listening Role-Play Exercise

Gather with friends or family and take turns sharing a story or concern. Practice active listening by maintaining eye contact, paraphrasing, and reflecting feelings. After each story, provide feedback on the listener's strengths and areas for improvement. This exercise helps solidify active listening skills in a supportive environment.

Incorporating active listening into daily interactions strengthens bonds and enhances communication. Whether it's a casual chat or a deep discussion, this practice transforms how we connect with others, fostering relationships built on empathy and understanding. Active listening is a gift we give to those we care about, turning simple exchanges into meaningful moments of connection.

Active Listening Role-Play Exercise

Engage in an interactive group activity to sharpen your active listening skills! Gather with friends or family and take turns sharing a story, concern, or personal experience. The listener's role is to practice active listening by:

- Maintaining eye contact

- Showing attentive body language

- Paraphrasing key points to show understanding

- Reflecting the speaker's emotions

After each story, the group provides feedback to the listener. Highlight what they did well and suggest ways they can improve. This fun and supportive exercise is perfect for strengthening communication skills, building empathy, and fostering deeper connections.

Notes for Feedback

Speaker's Story or Concern:

_____

_____

Listener's Strengths:

_____

_____

Areas for Improvement:

_____

_____

Try it out and see how much better you can listen!

Effective Communication: Saying What You Mean

Imagine a world where everyone said exactly what they meant, where words carried the weight of sincerity and clarity. Communication, at its most effective, is clear and direct. It's not about shouting to be heard but about expressing thoughts and feelings honestly and respectfully. This approach not only fosters understanding but also builds stronger connections. Think about a time when you were misunderstood. Perhaps you felt frustrated or even hurt. Effective communication can prevent these scenarios by ensuring that your message is received as intended. One powerful tool for achieving this is using "I" statements. Instead of saying, "You never listen to me," which can be accusatory, try, "I feel ignored when I'm not heard." This simple shift in wording focuses on your feelings rather than blaming the other person, paving the way for a more constructive conversation.

Articulating needs and desires without aggression or passivity is a skill worth cultivating. Assertive communication is about finding that sweet spot where you respect both your own needs and those of others. It involves expressing yourself confidently without being overbearing. Imagine you're at a group meeting, and your ideas are overshadowed. Instead of withdrawing or bulldozing over others, you might say, "I'd like to share my thoughts on this topic." This communicates your desire to contribute while respecting the group dynamic. Assertiveness is like playing a well-tuned instrument; it allows your voice to be heard harmoniously within the ensemble. It's about standing your ground gracefully, ensuring that your message is neither lost in silence nor overwhelmed by noise.

How we say things — our tone and word choice — profoundly impacts how our message is received. The tone is like the color in a painting, setting the mood and context for what's being communicated. A gentle tone can soften a difficult conversation, while a harsh one might escalate it unnecessarily. Similarly, word choice is the brushstroke that defines the message. Consider the difference between saying, "I need you to do this," versus, "Could you help me with this?" The former can sound like a command, while the latter invites cooperation. Choosing words thoughtfully creates a dialogue that invites understanding rather than conflict. This awareness of tone and language transforms everyday interactions, making them more meaningful and effective.

Practice is key to building confidence in communication. Role-playing exercises provide a safe environment to experiment with different approaches. Imagine a scenario where you need to discuss curfew with your parents. Practice expressing your viewpoint using "I" statements and assertive language. Role-play with friends or mentors who can offer feedback on your delivery and help you refine your approach. This exercise builds your confidence and equips you with the skills to handle real-life conversations with poise. As you practice, you'll notice a shift in how you express yourself, moving from tentative whispers to confident, clear communication.

Effective communication is a skill that opens doors to deeper understanding and connection. By expressing yourself clearly and directly, you invite others into your world, sharing not just words but the emotions and thoughts behind them. It's about creating a space where everyone feels heard and valued, where conversations become bridges rather than barriers. As you navigate the complexities of relationships, remember that your words have the power to connect, heal, and bring people closer together.

Empathy in Relationships: Walking in Their Shoes

Empathy acts like a bridge, connecting people across the chasm of misunderstanding. It's the ability to step into someone else's shoes, to see the world through their eyes, and feel their emotions as if they were your own. When you practice empathy, you're not just hearing words but also understanding the emotions and experiences behind them. This understanding can transform relationships, turning surface-level interactions into deep, meaningful connections. Imagine a friend sharing their struggles at home, and instead of merely nodding

83

along, you truly grasp the weight of their words. By acknowledging their pain and responding with compassion, you create a space where they feel supported and valued. It's like offering a hand to someone who's stumbling, helping them find their footing again.

Developing empathy is a skill that can be nurtured through practice. Perspective-taking is a powerful exercise that encourages you to consider situations from another's viewpoint. Picture a scenario where your sibling is upset over something you find trivial. Instead of dismissing their feelings, try to understand why it matters to them. Ask yourself, "How would I feel in their position?" This shift in perspective can open your eyes to their reality, fostering compassion and patience. Empathetic response practice is another technique to hone this skill. It involves actively listening to someone's concerns and responding in a way that reflects understanding and support. For instance, rather than saying, "You'll get over it," try, "That sounds really tough. How can I help?" These exercises help you develop a more nuanced understanding of others, strengthening your ability to connect on a deeper level.

It's important to distinguish between empathy and sympathy, as they play different roles in relationships. Sympathy often involves feeling pity for someone else's situation seeing their struggles from a distance. It's like watching a storm from the safety of your window. Empathy, on the other hand, is about stepping out into the rain, sharing in the experience and understanding the intensity of the storm. While sympathy can sometimes feel condescending, empathy builds a connection rooted in shared experiences and emotions. This distinction is crucial in relationships as it guides how you respond to others' feelings and challenges.

Reflecting on personal experiences of empathy can offer valuable insights into its impact. Think about a time when someone truly understood what you were going through. Maybe it was a friend who sat with you silently when words felt too heavy or a parent who listened without judgment as you poured out your worries. How did it make you feel? Chances are, it provided relief and comfort, knowing you weren't alone. These moments highlight the power of empathy to heal and connect, reinforcing its importance in relationships. Encourage teens to reflect on these experiences, considering how they felt understood and how it influenced their interactions with others. This reflection helps solidify the value of empathy, motivating them to practice it more consciously in their daily lives.

Interactive Element: Perspective-Taking Reflection

Take a moment to write about a recent situation where you felt misunderstood. Now, flip the script and consider how the other person might have felt. What might they have been thinking or experiencing? Reflect on how this new perspective changes your understanding of the situation. This exercise helps cultivate empathy by encouraging you to explore different viewpoints.

---

1. Reflecting on Your Experience

- Describe the situation where you felt misunderstood.

_____

_____

_____

- What emotions did I feel during this situation (e.g., frustration, sadness, confusion)?

_____

_____

_____

- Why do I think I was misunderstood? What was I trying to communicate?

_____

_____

_____

_____

2. Flipping the Script: The Other Person's Perspective

- How might the other person have been feeling during this situation?

_____

_____

_____

- What could they have been thinking or experiencing that influenced their response?

_____

_____

_____

- Were there any external factors or personal struggles that may have shaped their perspective?

_____

_____

_____

3. Gaining Insight from a New Perspective

- How does considering the other person's perspective change my understanding of the situation?

_____

_____

_____

- What lessons can I take away from this reflection about communication and empathy?

_____

_____

_____

_____

4. Moving Forward

- How might I approach similar situations differently in the future to avoid misunderstandings?

_____

_____

_____

- What steps can I take to foster better relationship understanding and connection?

_____

_____

_____

_____

Trust Building: The Foundation of Strong Bonds

Trust is like the bedrock of any relationship. Without it, even the strongest connections can crumble. Do you know how you need a solid foundation when building something? Trust is the foundation of relationships. It allows you to feel safe, knowing you can rely on someone, whether a friend, a parent, or a partner. Trust creates an environment where honesty and openness thrive, and misunderstandings are less likely to cause lasting damage. The glue holds people together, making navigating life's ups and downs easier.

Building trust isn't something that happens overnight, however. It requires consistent effort and commitment to specific behaviors that reinforce reliability. Actions like being honest, keeping promises, and showing up when you say you will all contribute to a culture of trust. Think about it—when someone consistently does what they say they'll do, it's easier to believe in them. Consistency builds confidence, and confidence breeds trust. It's like watering a plant; regular care leads to growth and strength. Every time you follow through on a promise, no matter how small, you nurture the trust between you and the other person.

But what happens when trust is broken? It's a challenging situation, for sure, but not an impossible one. Rebuilding trust takes time, patience, and, perhaps most importantly, accountability. Admitting when you're wrong and taking responsibility for your actions is the first step to repair the breach. It's like acknowledging that a storm has passed; now it's time to clean up the mess. Open dialogue about what happened and why it hurt is crucial. This isn't just about saying sorry; it's about understanding the impact of your actions and showing a genuine willingness to make amends. Forgiveness exercises can play a vital role here, helping both parties overcome the hurt and rebuild what was lost. Forgiving isn't about forgetting but about letting go of resentment to allow healing.

Maintaining trust is an ongoing process, a constant effort to keep the lines of communication open and clear. It's about being transparent about your intentions and feelings, ensuring that misunderstandings don't have a chance to take root. Think of it like tending to a garden; regularly check for weeds and nurture the plants to keep them healthy. Regular check-ins with those you care about can help reinforce trust, making sure everyone feels heard and understood. This doesn't have to be formal—just a simple "How are we doing?" can work wonders. It's a way to stay connected and ensure trust remains strong and intact.

Apology and Forgiveness Exercise

Take a moment to reflect on a time you may have broken someone's trust. Write a letter (that you don't have to send) expressing your understanding of the situation, your feelings, and how you plan to make amends. Then, write a second letter to yourself, forgiving your mistakes and acknowledging your growth. This exercise encourages accountability and self-compassion, two key elements in rebuilding trust.

Apology and Forgiveness Exercise

Reflect on a moment when you may have broken someone's trust. This exercise is about fostering accountability and self-compassion as you work through the experience.

1. **Write an Apology Letter**

Compose a letter (that you don't need to send) to the person involved. In the letter:

- o Acknowledge what happened and your role in the situation.
- o Express your feelings about the impact it may have had on them.
- o Share how you plan to make amends and prevent a similar situation.

2. **Write a Forgiveness Letter to Yourself**

Next, write a letter to yourself. In this letter:

- o Recognize your mistakes with honesty.
- o Acknowledge your steps to grow and learn from the experience.
- o Offer yourself forgiveness and kindness as you move forward.

These letters are for your eyes only. They are a safe space to process emotions and reflect on your growth.

Notes for Reflection

Apology Letter

- **What happened and your role:**

_____

_____

Impact on the other person:

_____

_____

- **Plan for making amends:**

_____

_____

Forgiveness Letter to Yourself

- **Recognized mistakes and lessons learned:**

_____

_____

- **Steps taken for growth and self-improvement:**

_____

_____

- **Words of self-compassion:**

_____

_____

This practice allows you to process emotions and rebuild trust with others and yourself. Take your time, and let the writing guide your healing journey.

Setting Boundaries: Respecting Yourself and Others

Setting boundaries is like drawing a map of your personal space, marking where you feel comfortable and safe. Imagine it as having an invisible fence that safeguards your emotional well-being and promotes mutual respect. These boundaries are crucial because they define your limits, helping others understand how to interact with you. They can be emotional, physical, or digital. Emotional boundaries relate to your feelings and energy, defining what you're willing to share and how you expect to be treated. Physical boundaries involve your personal space and physical contact, ensuring you're comfortable with how others interact with you. Digital boundaries pertain to your online presence, such as who can contact you and what personal information you want to share on social media. Establishing these boundaries is vital for maintaining healthy relationships and ensuring that interactions remain respectful and fulfilling.

Articulating your boundaries can sometimes feel challenging, especially if you're not used to asserting yourself. However, it's essential to communicate them clearly and respectfully. This means using straightforward language that leaves no room for ambiguity. For example, if you need time alone to recharge, you might say, "I need some quiet time right now. Can we talk later?" or if someone is pressuring you to share something personal, you might assert, "I'm not comfortable discussing that at the moment." The key is to express your needs without aggression, clarifying why these boundaries are important to you. This approach protects your well-being and teaches others how to respect your limits, paving the way for healthier interactions.

Equally important is respecting the boundaries of others. Just as you have your personal space and limits, so do those around you. Mutual respect is the cornerstone of any healthy relationship. When someone sets a boundary, it's crucial to honor it, even if you don't fully understand or agree. This respect shows that you value their needs and are willing to try to maintain a healthy relationship. For instance, if a friend tells you they need time alone, respect their request without taking it personally. Doing so demonstrates a level of maturity and understanding that strengthens your bond. It's saying, "I respect you enough to honor your needs," which fosters trust and mutual respect.

Practicing boundary negotiation can be valuable, especially in scenarios where boundaries might conflict. Role-playing is an effective way to get comfortable with this process. Picture a scenario where you and a sibling share a room and need to negotiate personal space. Practice expressing your needs, like saying, "I need a quiet space to study from 7 to 9 PM," while listening to their needs. This exercise encourages open dialogue, teaching you to navigate situations where compromise is necessary. It's about balancing both parties' boundaries, ensuring everyone feels heard and respected. The more you practice, the more natural it becomes to assert your boundaries in real-life situations.

Boundaries are about creating a safe space for yourself and others. They're not walls meant to shut people out but guidelines encouraging healthier interactions. Setting and respecting boundaries fosters an environment where everyone feels valued and understood. This practice is integral to maintaining emotional well-being and building strong, respectful relationships.

Repairing Relationships: After the Storm

When relationships hit rough patches, it can feel like you're standing in the aftermath of a storm, unsure where to begin picking up the pieces. Reconciliation starts with understanding the root cause of conflict. Disputes often arise from misunderstandings, unmet expectations, or deeper issues brewing beneath the surface. Identifying these core issues is crucial. It's like peeling back layers to reveal what's driving the discord. This might involve reflecting on past interactions and considering how each party's actions and words contributed to the tension. Sometimes, it helps to step back and ask yourself what is fueling the disagreement. Is it a specific incident, or are there underlying feelings of resentment or hurt that must be addressed? Understanding the trustworthy source of conflict lays the groundwork for healing and moving forward together.

Once the root cause is identified, the next step is directly addressing the issue, using conflict resolution strategies that foster healing. Mediation can be particularly effective, especially in situations where emotions run high. This involves having a neutral third party facilitate the discussion, ensuring both sides are heard and understood. It's like having a referee who can guide the conversation constructively, helping to keep emotions in check and focus on solutions. Negotiation exercises are another valuable tool, where both parties come together to discuss their needs and work towards a compromise. Picture a scenario where siblings disagree over shared responsibilities at home. They can find a resolution that respects both their needs by sitting down and negotiating a fair division of tasks. These strategies promote collaboration, turning conflict into an opportunity for growth and understanding.

Forgiveness plays a pivotal role in the healing process. It's about letting go of grudges and resentment, allowing space for renewal and connection. Forgiving others and yourself is not about forgetting past hurts but acknowledging them and choosing to move past them. It's like releasing a heavy weight you've been carrying, freeing yourself to embrace the present with an open heart. This process requires patience and understanding, both from those who have been hurt and those who have caused hurt. It can be helpful to engage in forgiveness exercises, where you reflect on the situation, acknowledge the pain, and consciously decide to let it go. This act of forgiveness is integral to rebuilding trust and ensuring the relationship can flourish again.

Repairing relationships also demands ongoing communication and consistent effort. Healing doesn't happen overnight; it's a continuous rebuilding process that strengthens the once-strained bonds. Regular check-ins provide open dialogue, allowing both parties to express their feelings and progress. Imagine touching base with a friend after a disagreement, discussing how things have been and any lingering concerns. This ongoing communication fosters transparency, ensuring that minor issues are addressed before they become more significant conflicts. It's like tending to a garden; regular care and attention help it thrive. By committing to this effort, you reinforce the commitment to the relationship, showing that it's worth investing in.

As you work through these steps, remember that repairing relationships requires a genuine desire to heal and reconnect. The effort you invest in mending broken bonds can lead to deeper, more meaningful connections. It's a reminder that even after the storm, there's always a chance for renewal, growth, and a stronger foundation. The journey of reconciliation can be challenging, but it also offers an opportunity to learn, grow, and strengthen the ties that matter most.

Chapter 5: Navigating Social and Academic Pressures

Balancing Expectations, Self-Worth, and the Stress of Teen Life

Picture yourself sitting at your desk, a pile of textbooks to one side, a laptop open to your latest assignment, and a calendar filled with sticky notes reminding you of looming deadlines. It's a familiar scene for many teens, a silent reminder of the academic pressures that can feel overwhelming. The expectations of juggling homework, preparing for exams, and maintaining good grades can weigh heavily on your shoulders, sometimes leaving you gasping for air. It's not just about the grades but the anxiety that creeps in during exam periods, turning your nights restless and your days stressful.

Test anxiety is a real challenge that many face. The pressure to perform well can lead to sleepless nights and a racing heart as you enter the exam room. It's like standing on a stage, knowing all eyes are on you, and your mind suddenly goes blank. This anxiety can affect your ability to concentrate and recall information, making exams more daunting than they need to be. Coupled with the ever-growing mountain of homework, the stress can feel insurmountable, like trying to climb a peak that keeps growing taller with every step.

Time management becomes your best ally in conquering these academic stressors. It involves organizing and prioritizing tasks to use your time effectively. A daily study schedule can help you allocate specific time slots for different subjects or projects, ensuring you cover everything without feeling rushed. It's like having a roadmap that guides you through your day, reducing the chaos and providing a sense of control. The Eisenhower Box is another effective tool, helping you prioritize tasks based on urgency and importance. By focusing on what truly matters, you can avoid the trap of procrastination and make steady progress.

Setting up a conducive study environment is equally important. Imagine focusing in a cluttered room where every item competes for your attention. A tidy, well-organized space can significantly enhance your focus and productivity. Keep your desk free of distractions, with only the essentials within reach. Good lighting and a comfortable chair also make a difference, turning your study area into a haven for concentration. It's about creating a space that invites focus and minimizes interruptions, allowing you to dive deep into your work.

Study aids and resources are like the secret weapons in your academic arsenal. Flashcards and online quizzes can reinforce what you've learned, making it easier to retain information. They offer a fun and interactive way to test your knowledge, breaking the monotony of traditional study methods. These tools are invaluable for visual learners, who benefit from seeing information laid out in a clear, concise manner. By incorporating these aids, you can transform your study sessions from a chore into an engaging experience.

Interactive Element: Personal Study Space Checklist

Use the checklist below to evaluate and optimize your study space. Includes elements such as lighting, organization, and comfort. Adjust and enhance your environment for better focus and productivity.

Navigating the pressures of school requires a blend of strategy, organization, and self-care. By managing your time effectively, creating a supportive study environment, and utilizing study aids, you arm yourself against the stressors of academic life. These skills help you succeed academically and build resilience and confidence, preparing you for the challenges ahead.

Personal Study Space Checklist

Use this checklist to evaluate and optimize your study space for better focus and productivity.

---

1. Lighting

- Is the lighting bright enough to prevent eye strain?

- Is there access to natural light during the day?

- Are there adjustable lamps for evening study sessions?

- Are there any harsh glares or shadows that might distract me?

---

2. Organization

- Are all my study materials (books, pens, notebooks) within easy reach?

- Do I have designated spots for essential items (e.g., chargers, calculators)?

- Is the space free of unnecessary clutter?

- Do I have shelves, drawers, or organizers to keep things tidy?

- Can I quickly find the materials I need without wasting time?

---

3. Comfort

- Is my chair supportive and adjustable for proper posture?

- Is my desk at a comfortable height for writing or typing?

- Do I have a cushion or back support if needed?

- Is the room temperature comfortable for extended periods of focus?

- Are there distractions (e.g., noise, uncomfortable surfaces) I need to address?

---

4. Technology

- Is my computer, laptop, or tablet set up ergonomically?

- Are all necessary devices fully charged or near an outlet?

- Do I have reliable internet access?

- Are study apps, timers, or digital resources ready to use?

- Have I minimized notifications or digital distractions?

---

5. Atmosphere and Personalization

- Is the space inviting and motivational (e.g., posters, quotes, plants)?

- Do I have a way to play soft background music or white noise if needed?

- Are there personal touches that make the space feel comfortable?

- Is there a balance between being visually interesting but not overwhelming?

---

6. Time Management Tools

- Do I have a clock or timer to help manage my study sessions?

- Is my planner or calendar accessible to track tasks and deadlines?

- Have I set up a to-do list or schedule for the day?

---

7. Break and Self-Care Essentials

- Is there water or healthy snacks nearby to stay hydrated and energized?

- Do I have a comfortable spot for short breaks?

- Have I set a timer or reminder to take regular study breaks?

- Are there relaxation tools (e.g., stress ball, fidget spinner) if I need them?

Bonus: Quick Tips to Enhance Your Study Environment

- Clear your desk before and after each study session.

- Keep only what you need for the task at hand.

- Test your setup regularly to adjust.

Social Media Savvy: Navigating Online Interactions

Today's social media is like a bustling city square where everyone has something to say. For many teens, it's the place to catch up with friends, share life's highlights, and sometimes seek validation. The impact of likes and comments can profoundly shape how you view yourself. A single post can generate a cascade of likes, offering a fleeting boost of confidence or sitting unnoticed, casting a shadow of self-doubt. This rollercoaster of emotions is familiar, as online interactions often become a mirror reflecting a curated image of self-worth. But it's crucial to remember that self-esteem shouldn't be tied solely to digital approval. Finding a balance where online feedback complements self-worth rather than defines it can be a liberating shift.

Understanding digital literacy and critical thinking is key to navigating this online world effectively. It's about knowing how to evaluate what you see and recognizing reliable sources from misleading ones. Think of it as developing a filter that helps you sift through vast information. When you encounter an article or post, ask yourself: Who wrote this? What's their motive? Is there evidence to support their claims? By questioning the credibility of sources, you become an informed participant in the digital landscape. Understanding digital footprints is essential—every click, share, and like leaves a trace. Awareness of this can guide you in making conscious choices about what you share, knowing it contributes to your online persona.

Maintaining healthy online relationships involves more than just liking and commenting. It requires setting boundaries that protect your privacy and well-being. Start by adjusting privacy controls on your social media accounts. Decide who can see your posts, who can contact you, and what information is visible to others. This safeguards personal details and creates a space to interact more comfortably. Strategies for dealing with cyberbullying are equally important. If you encounter negativity, remember it's okay to block or mute users who make you uncomfortable. Don't hesitate to contact trusted friends, family, or school counselors for support. Engaging positively online means fostering connections that uplift and inspire rather than diminish.

Balancing online interactions with offline experiences is critical for a well-rounded social life. While social media connects you with friends far and wide, real-world connections nurture more profound, meaningful relationships. Make time for activities that don't involve screens, like meeting up with friends for a hike or attending a local event. These offline interactions around you remind you of the joys of face-to-face conversations and shared experiences. They offer a respite from the digital buzz, allowing you to be present in the moment. In this blended world, cultivating a balance between online and offline connections ensures you enjoy the best of both realms.

Interactive Element: Online Self-Reflection Exercise

Reflect on your social media habits. Consider which interactions uplift you and which drain your energy. Use this insight to create a digital space that aligns with your values, fostering positive connections that enhance your self-image and well-being.

Navigating social media with awareness and intention can transform how you interact with the digital world. By cultivating critical thinking, setting boundaries, and fostering real-world connections, you create a balanced social experience that supports your growth and happiness.

Online Self-Reflection Exercise: Social Media Habits

Take a moment to reflect on your social media use. Use the following prompts and lines to journal your thoughts:

1. Reflecting on Your Habits

- How much time do I spend on social media daily or weekly?

_____

_____

_____

- What emotions do I typically feel after using social media (e.g., joy, envy, frustration)?

_____

_____

_____

_____

2. Identifying Positive Interactions

- Which accounts or interactions uplift, inspire, or make me feel positive?

_____

_____

_____

- How do these positive interactions contribute to my self-esteem or personal growth?

_____

_____

_____

_____

3. Recognizing Negative Influences

- What types of content, accounts, or interactions drain my energy or negatively impact my self-image?

_____

_____

_____

- Why do I continue engaging with these accounts or content, and what steps can I take to limit exposure?

_____

_____

_____

_____

4. Aligning Your Digital Space with Your Values

- What are my core values, and how can my social media habits better align with them?

_____

_____

_____

- What steps can I take to curate a digital space that fosters positivity and self-growth?

_____

_____

_____

_____

5. Action Plan for a Healthier Relationship with Social Media

- What boundaries can I set for social media use (e.g., time limits, specific apps)?

_____

_____

_____

- What kind of connections or communities do I want to foster online?

_____

_____

_____

_____

Peer Approval vs. Self-Approval: Finding Balance

Imagine walking into school, the halls buzzing with chatter, and feeling that familiar tug—the need to fit in. It's a natural feeling, especially during the teen years, when being part of a group can seem like the most important thing. Peer approval often feels like a ticket to acceptance, a way to blend in and avoid standing out as different. This desire to fit in can sometimes lead to social conformity, where choices are influenced more by what others think than personal beliefs. You might dress a certain way, listen to specific music, or alter your behavior to align with the group. While this can provide a sense of belonging, knowing how it affects your behavior and decisions is crucial.

However, while fitting in can seem important, it's equally vital to nurture self-approval. This means cultivating a sense of self-worth and confidence that isn't dependent on external validation. Self-acceptance and personal integrity are the cornerstones of a fulfilling life. When your actions align with your values, it's like finding a compass that guides you through life's twists and turns. Consider the benefits of living authentically: less stress from trying to please everyone, more confidence in your decisions, and a deeper understanding of who you are. Aligning your actions with your values creates peace and satisfaction, allowing you to stand firm even when external pressures try to sway you.

Resisting peer pressure is a skill that can be developed with practice. It requires the ability to maintain individuality while still fostering healthy relationships. One effective method is role-playing scenarios where you practice saying no. This exercise can be as simple as imagining a situation where friends pressure you to do something uncomfortable. Practice responding firmly and calmly, using clear language to express your boundaries. Rehearsing these scenarios builds the confidence to assert yourself in real-life situations. It's about standing your ground and staying true to yourself, even when it feels challenging. This doesn't mean isolating yourself from others but finding friends who respect your choices and encourage your growth.

Self-reflection is a powerful tool for personal growth and self-discovery. It involves taking the time to set individual goals that reflect your true self. These goals should be based on your interests, passions, and values rather than what others expect of you. Consider what makes you happy and fulfilled, and use that as a foundation for setting your objectives. Regularly checking in with yourself to assess your progress and make necessary adjustments is key. This practice helps you grow as an individual and strengthens your ability to navigate life's complexities with confidence and clarity. By focusing on your personal growth, you create a life that resonates with your authentic self, free from the constraints of external approval.

Striking a balance is crucial in this intricate dance between peer approval and self-approval. It's about embracing your uniqueness while connecting with others meaningfully. This balance empowers you to live authentically, making choices that reflect your identity. As you cultivate self-approval, you build a solid foundation of self-worth and confidence that supports you in all aspects of life. Ultimately, this journey of self-discovery leads to a deeper understanding of yourself and the world around you, allowing you to thrive amidst the ever-changing landscape of adolescence.

Extracurricular Overload: Prioritizing Passions

Imagine diving into a pool of endless possibilities where every club and team calls your name. At first, being involved in sports, drama, band, and debate is exhilarating. But soon, what seemed like a sea of opportunities can turn into a whirlpool of commitments, each pulling you in different directions. The thrill of being active and engaged in multiple extracurricular activities is undeniable. They offer a platform to hone skills, make friends, and explore interests beyond academics. But there's a flip side. Juggling too many activities can lead to burnout, where the joy of participation gets overshadowed by the stress of over-commitment. It's like trying to keep a dozen plates spinning at once—eventually, something's bound to crash.

Balancing sports, clubs, and academics becomes a high-wire act. Each demands time and energy, and when stretched too thin, you risk losing the spark that drew you to them in the first place. It's important to recognize when you're taking on too much. This realization is the first step towards creating a healthier balance. Think of your commitments as a garden. Initially, you might plant various seeds, eager to see what grows. But as time passes, you learn which plants thrive and bring you joy and which require more effort than they're worth. Prioritizing your passions helps you focus on what truly matters, allowing you to nurture those interests that align with your long-term goals and values.

One effective way to manage this is by creating a priority list of your extracurriculars. List all your activities and rank them based on how much they fulfill you and how they contribute to your future aspirations. This exercise helps clarify which activities deserve more time and which might be pruned back. It's about making conscious choices that serve your well-being. Once you've identified your priorities, the next step is to implement time management strategies. Schedule specific times for each activity, ensuring you allocate enough time for rest. Downtime is crucial. It's not wasted time but an opportunity to recharge and reflect. Just as athletes need rest days to perform at their best, you need moments of calm to maintain your enthusiasm and energy.

Encouraging the exploration of new interests is also vital. It's easy to fall into a routine, sticking with activities simply because they're familiar. But stepping out of your comfort zone can lead to unexpected discoveries. Trying new things can reveal hidden talents and passions you never knew you had. Maybe you've always assumed you wouldn't enjoy painting, but a workshop at your local community center sparks a newfound love for art. Or perhaps volunteering at a local shelter introduces you to a passion for helping others. These explorations can be refreshing and invigorating, offering new perspectives and opportunities for growth.

The key to avoiding extracurricular overload lies in balance and self-awareness. You create a fulfilling and sustainable schedule by understanding your limits and prioritizing your passions. It's about finding harmony between doing what you love and maintaining your well-being. Remember, it's okay to say no sometimes. Deciding to focus on fewer activities doesn't mean you're missing out; it means you're making room for what enriches your life.

Handling Bullying: Standing Up for Yourself

Bullying is a term often thrown around, but its impact can be profoundly personal and lasting. It's not just about the physical confrontations that may come to mind first; bullying can take many forms, each with its own set of challenges. Physical bullying involves any form of physical aggression, from pushing to more severe acts of violence. Verbal bullying, on the other hand, includes taunts, threats, and hurtful words that can leave invisible scars. Then there's cyberbullying, a more modern menace, where the anonymity of the internet allows bullies to harass their victims with words and images that can spread quickly and linger online. Recognizing cyberbullying can sometimes be tricky since it doesn't happen in plain view and can manifest through consistent negative comments, exclusion from online groups, or the spread of false information. These various forms of bullying all share a common trait: they can profoundly affect your emotional well-being, leading to feelings of isolation, fear, and helplessness.

Empowering yourself to address bullying starts with understanding the importance of assertive communication. This doesn't mean responding aggressively but standing firm in your own space and expressing your feelings and boundaries clearly. Imagine planting your feet on solid ground, unshaken by the storm around you. When confronted by a bully, you might say, "I don't appreciate your comments; please stop," using a calm yet firm tone. This approach communicates that you will not tolerate disrespect without escalating the situation. In severe cases, reporting bullying to authorities, whether a teacher, school counselor or even law enforcement, is another critical step. It's not about tattling; it's about ensuring safety and support. Schools often have protocols to handle such situations, and reaching out can lead to understanding and action that might not happen if bullying is kept hidden.

Support networks are lifelines in these situations. Friends, family, and mentors can provide the understanding and encouragement you need to face bullying. They offer a listening ear, advice, and sometimes even intervene on your behalf. Imagine your support network as a circle of strength around you, helping to buffer the impact of bullying. Talking to someone you trust can also help you process your emotions, making the burden a little lighter. It's about knowing you're not alone and that others care about your well-being. Reaching out to a trusted adult can sometimes feel daunting, but it's a step toward creating a safe environment where you feel valued and protected. These connections can remind you of your worth and potential, offering hope and perspective when things feel overwhelming.

Building resilience and self-confidence is crucial in overcoming the challenges posed by bullying. Resilience is the ability to bounce back from adversity and rise after being knocked down. It involves developing a strong sense of self-worth and belief in your abilities, which can act as armor against the negativity of bullies. Engaging in activities you excel at or enjoy can help build this inner strength. Whether it's sports, arts, or academics, finding something that makes you feel accomplished can boost your confidence. Surrounding yourself with positive influences affirming your values can bolster your self-esteem. These supportive relationships can act as mirrors, reflecting the qualities that make you unique and valuable. Remember, resilience isn't about never falling but about having the courage to stand up each time you do.

Future Focus: Planning Without Panic

Imagining the future can feel like standing at the edge of a vast, uncharted ocean. The possibilities stretch out before you, endless and sometimes overwhelming. Getting caught up in the uncertainty of what lies ahead is easy, but setting goals can offer a sense of direction and purpose. Think of goal-setting as plotting a course on a map; it helps confidently guide you through the unknown. When you know where you're headed, the journey becomes less daunting and more like an adventure waiting to unfold. Creating a vision board can be a fun and inspiring way to visualize your aspirations. Collect images, quotes, and symbols representing your dreams, and arrange them on a board to keep your goals in sight. This visual reminder is a daily nudge to stay focused and motivated, even when the path seems uncertain.

The SMART framework is a powerful tool for crafting inspiring and achievable goals. SMART stands for Specific, Measurable, Achievable, Relevant, and Time-bound. Start by setting short-term goals as stepping stones toward your larger aspirations. For example, if your long-term goal is to become a veterinarian, a short-term goal could be volunteering at an animal shelter. Make sure your goals are clear and measurable so you can track your progress and celebrate small victories along the way. This approach breaks down the bigger picture into manageable pieces, making it easier to stay on track and avoid feeling overwhelmed. It's like climbing a mountain one step at a time; each step brings you closer to the summit.

Uncertainty is a natural part of life; learning to cope with it is crucial for your well-being. Mindfulness practices offer a way to anchor yourself in the present moment, reducing anxiety about the future. When you practice mindfulness, you focus on what you can control right now rather than worrying about what might happen later. Simple techniques like deep breathing, meditation, or even a mindful walk can help clear your mind and bring a sense of calm. This clarity allows you to adapt more quickly to changes and unexpected challenges, making you more resilient in the face of uncertainty. It's about finding peace in the present, even when the future feels unpredictable.

Exploring career and educational options is an exciting part of planning for the future. It's a chance to discover what truly interests and excites you. Start by researching different fields and talking to those working in those areas. Internships, job shadowing, and informational interviews can provide valuable insights into potential careers. Consider your strengths and passions and consider how they align with various paths. This exploration isn't about making a final decision immediately but gathering information to make informed choices. It's like sampling different flavors before deciding on your favorite ice cream; each experience adds to your understanding of what you enjoy and excel at.

As we conclude this chapter, remember that planning for the future is not about having all the answers right now. It's about laying a foundation for growth and discovery. Setting goals, embracing uncertainty, and exploring new opportunities create a roadmap that guides you forward. This journey of self-discovery and planning is crucial to building a life that reflects your values and dreams. In the next chapter, we'll delve into building resilience and confidence, essential tools for navigating the twists and turns of life with grace and strength.

Chapter 6: Building Resilience and Confidence

Bridge the Gap, Build Understanding, and Work Together

Have you ever watched a tree bend in the wind, its branches swaying yet never breaking? That's resilience in action. It's the capacity to withstand and recover quickly from difficulties, much like that tree that stands tall and rooted despite the storm. Resilience isn't just about enduring; it's about thriving in adversity. Challenges come at us from every angle—school pressures, social dynamics, and family changes. Bouncing back is crucial for surviving these storms and emerging stronger and wiser. Emotional fortitude is the inner strength that helps you navigate these challenges without being overwhelmed. It's like having a mental toolkit filled with strategies for coping with whatever life throws your way.

Resilient individuals often share specific characteristics that set them apart. Adaptability is one of those traits. Life is unpredictable, and those who can adjust to new situations without losing their footing are better equipped to handle change. Think of adaptability as your internal GPS, recalculating the route when you hit a roadblock. Persistence is another key quality. It's the determination to keep going, even when the path gets tough. Picture someone climbing a steep hill; each step is difficult, but each is also progress. Optimism, the ability to see potential good in every situation, fuels this persistence. It's the light that guides you when the way forward seems dark. Together, these traits form a robust foundation for resilience, enabling individuals to face challenges confidently and gracefully.

Cultivating resilience offers numerous benefits, particularly for mental health and overall life satisfaction. Resilient people tend to experience lower levels of stress and anxiety because they have the tools to manage their emotions effectively. This improved mental health leads to a greater sense of life satisfaction, as individuals feel more in control and capable of handling whatever comes their way.

Resilience also promotes a positive outlook, encouraging you to view setbacks as growth opportunities rather than failures. This perspective shift can transform how you approach challenges, turning them into learning experiences that contribute to personal development and well-being.

Developing resilience involves practicing certain habits that strengthen your ability to cope with life's ups and downs. Practicing gratitude is a simple yet powerful method. By focusing on the things you're thankful for, you shift your attention from what's going wrong to what's going right, fostering a positive mindset. Try keeping a gratitude journal, jotting down three daily things that bring you joy. Positive thinking also plays a crucial role. It's not about ignoring problems but approaching them with a mindset toward solutions. Engaging in problem-solving exercises can enhance this skill. When faced with a challenge, break it into smaller, manageable parts and brainstorm potential solutions. This approach builds confidence in your ability to tackle problems and reinforces the belief that you can overcome obstacles.

Interactive Element: Resilience Reflection Exercise

Take a moment to reflect on a recent challenge you faced. Write about how you handled it and what you learned from the experience. Consider the traits of resilience—adaptability, persistence, optimism—and how they played a role in your response. What could you do differently next time? This exercise helps you recognize your resilience in action and identify areas for growth.

Resilience is a skill you can cultivate over time, much like a muscle that strengthens with use. Focusing on gratitude, positive thinking, and problem-solving builds a foundation that supports emotional fortitude and adaptability. These practices empower you to navigate life's challenges confidently, turning setbacks into stepping stones for growth and learning. Resilience doesn't make life easier, but it makes you stronger, equipping you with the tools to face adversity and emerge even more capable than before.

Positive Self-Talk: Rewriting Your Inner Dialogue

Have you ever thought, "I'm just not good enough," after a bad day? That internal chatter, or self-talk, plays a massive role in how you see yourself and the world around you. Positive self-talk is like having a cheerleader in your mind, boosting your confidence and motivation. Conversely, negative self-talk can be a relentless critic, eroding your self-esteem and outlook. Imagine waking up to a day filled with possibilities, only to have your inner voice say, "You'll never be able to do it." It sets the tone for how you tackle challenges, often making them seem insurmountable before you've even begun.

Recognizing when negative self-talk creeps in is the first step to transforming it. These thought patterns often hide in plain sight, surfacing in moments of stress or self-doubt. Start by listening to your inner dialogue during challenging situations. Is it supportive, or does it default to criticism? Identifying these negative thought triggers can be as enlightening as uncomfortable, but it's necessary for change. Once you're aware, you can reframe these thoughts with positive affirmations. Instead of "I can't handle this," try saying, "I have the strength to figure this out." It sounds simple, but this shift can make a world of difference. You gradually retrain your brain to adopt a more positive, encouraging stance by consistently replacing negative thoughts with affirmations.

Treating yourself with kindness is crucial. Self-compassion means acknowledging that everyone, including you, has off days and makes mistakes. It's about giving yourself the same understanding and patience you'd offer a friend. When you fall short of your expectations, instead of being harsh, remind yourself that imperfection is part of being human. Think of self-compassion as a soft place to land after a hard day. It doesn't mean ignoring areas where you can improve but not beating yourself up. This practice nurtures resilience and fosters a healthier relationship with yourself, making it easier to bounce back from setbacks.

To make positive self-talk a habit, establish a routine of daily affirmations. You might start each morning by writing encouraging statements on sticky notes and placing them where you see them— like your mirror or computer screen. These affirmations should be personal, reflecting what you need most. For example, "I am capable" or "I am worthy of success" can be daily reminders of your strengths and potential. Crafting personalized affirmation lists is empowering, giving you ownership over your narrative. As these affirmations become a regular part of your day, they help reinforce self-belief and confidence.

Interactive Element: Affirmation Creation Exercise

Set aside time to create a list of personalized affirmations. Consider areas where you need encouragement and write statements that resonate with you. Reflect on them each morning and evening, noticing how they influence your thoughts and feelings over time.

Rewriting your inner dialogue through positive self-talk isn't about ignoring reality; it's about changing your perspective to see challenges as opportunities rather than obstacles. By shifting your self-talk, you cultivate a mindset that supports your growth and well-being. This isn't a quick fix but becomes a powerful tool for building self-confidence and resilience with practice. As you continue this practice, you'll find that the way you speak to yourself becomes more encouraging, helping you to face each day with renewed optimism and strength.

Daily Affirmation Practice Guide

This guide will help you incorporate affirmations into your daily routine, fostering positivity, resilience, and growth. Use it every morning and evening for consistent practice that rewires your inner dialogue.

Step 1: Set Your Intentions

Start by choosing affirmations that resonate with your personal goals and challenges. Below are examples you can use or adapt:

Morning Affirmations

- **Self-Worth:** *"I am worthy of success and happiness."*

- **Resilience:** *"I can handle anything that comes my way today."*

- **Growth:** *"Today is an opportunity to learn and grow."*

- **Gratitude:** *"I am grateful for this fresh start and the opportunities ahead."*

Evening Affirmations

- **Reflection:** *"I am proud of my efforts today, no matter how small."*

- **Emotional Balance:** *"I release today's worries and welcome peace."*

- **Gratitude:** *"I am thankful for the positive moments I experienced today."*

- **Strength:** *"I trust my ability to improve and move forward."*

Step 2: Personalize Your Affirmations

Take a moment to write affirmations tailored to your current needs. Use the space below:

- Morning Affirmations:

_____

_____

_____

- Evening Affirmations:

_____

_____

_____

Step 3: Create a Daily Routine

Use the following routine to integrate affirmations into your life:

1. **Morning Reflection (5–10 minutes):**

   o Find a quiet space.

   o Read your morning affirmations aloud with intention.

   o Take a few deep breaths, visualizing a joyous, productive day.

2. **Throughout the Day:**

   o Place affirmations where you'll see them: mirrors, desks, or phone screens.

o   When facing challenges, repeat an affirmation that encourages resilience.

3. **Evening Reflection (5–10 minutes):**

    o   Sit in a calm space and reflect on your day.

    o   Read your evening affirmations aloud.

    o   Write a brief journal entry about how your affirmations influenced your thoughts or actions.

Step 4: Track Your Progress

Use the prompts below to reflect weekly on your affirmation practice:

•   Which affirmation resonated with me the most this week?

_____

_____

•   How have my thoughts or feelings shifted since starting this practice?

_____

_____

- What challenges did I face, and how did affirmations help me?

_____

_____

- What new affirmations can I add for the upcoming week?

_____

_____

_____

Bonus Tips for Success

- **Consistency is key:** Commit to this practice daily, even for a few minutes.

- **Believe in your words:** Speak affirmations confidently, even if they initially feel unfamiliar.

- **Celebrate progress:** Acknowledge small shifts in your mindset and behavior.

Setting Realistic Goals: Steps to Success

Imagine standing at the base of a mountain, looking up at the peak. It seems daunting, right? That's what life's challenges can feel like without a plan. Setting realistic goals is like mapping out a trail to that summit. It provides direction and motivation, making the climb less intimidating. Goals act as guideposts, leading you step by step toward your destination. They're crucial because they give you something to aim for, something tangible to achieve. Short-term goals are like the rest stops along the way, providing quick wins and keeping your spirits up. Think of getting a passing grade on a quiz, which boosts your confidence for the final exam. Long-term goals, on the other hand, are the peak itself. They require more time and effort, like aiming for a college scholarship or mastering a musical instrument. Both types of goals are important. They work together, creating a path that guides your journey.

The SMART goals framework is a powerful tool for making these goals more effective. SMART stands for Specific, Measurable, Achievable, Relevant, and Time-bound. It's a method that transforms vague intentions into clear, actionable plans. Let's break it down: A specific goal identifies precisely what you want to achieve, leaving no room for ambiguity. For instance, instead of saying, "I want to do better in math," you might say, "I will improve my math grade by one letter by the end of the semester through weekly tutoring." Measurable goals allow you to track progress, providing feedback on how close you are to your target. Achievable goals are realistic, pushing you just enough without setting you up for failure. Relevance ties the goal to your broader life objectives, ensuring it contributes to your long-term vision. Finally, time-bound goals have deadlines, creating a sense of urgency and focus.

Breaking down significant goals into smaller tasks can make them more manageable. It's like dividing the mountain into smaller hills. Each hill conquered adds to your momentum, eventually leading you to the peak. Start by creating a step-by-step action plan. Let's say your goal is to write a novel. Begin with a timeline for drafting, revising, and editing. Break that timeline into daily or weekly writing targets, such as writing 500 words a day or a chapter a week. Each task should feel achievable, giving you a sense of accomplishment with every completion. This approach keeps you organized and reduces the feeling of being overwhelmed by a massive goal. The key is to celebrate each small victory; it fuels your determination to keep going, even when the going gets tough.

Flexibility is an essential part of goal setting. Life is unpredictable, and sometimes, things don't go as planned. Being adaptable means you're open to adjusting your goals as needed. Maybe you experience a setback, like an injury that disrupts your training schedule or a family emergency that demands your attention. Instead of abandoning your goals, consider revising them. Perhaps you need to extend your timeline or adjust your expectations. Flexibility doesn't mean you're giving up; you're navigating the changes with resilience. Your goals should serve you, not the other way around. You keep moving forward by staying adaptable, even if the path looks different from what you originally envisioned.

Setting realistic goals is a dynamic process. It requires a balance of ambition and practicality, vision and adaptability. When you approach goal setting with this mindset, you unlock a powerful tool for personal growth. It's a way to chart your course, one step at a time, as you climb toward your dreams.

Celebrating Small Wins: Building Momentum

In a world that often feels like it's spinning too fast, it's easy to overlook the small victories. Yet, these small wins are like the stepping stones that lead us across the river of life. They might seem insignificant initially, but acknowledging these achievements can fuel your motivation and confidence. Celebrating small accomplishments isn't about patting yourself on the back for every little thing but recognizing your progress. Each step forward brings you closer to your larger goals, no matter how minor. Think of it like climbing a mountain; each foothold you secure is a triumph, making the summit feel possible and inevitable.

Tracking your progress is a powerful way to keep your momentum going. A success journal can become your record of achievements, big and small. Each entry serves as a reminder of what you've accomplished and the effort it took to get there. It might be as simple as jotting down that you finally spoke up in class or managed a difficult conversation with a friend. Over time, this journal becomes a testament to your growth, a resource you can turn to when self-doubt creeps in. Another effective method is creating a reward system for reaching milestones. This doesn't mean splurging on something extravagant whenever you check off a task. It's about giving yourself something to look forward to—a favorite snack, a movie night, or extra time spent on a hobby you love. These rewards reinforce the idea that hard work pays off, encouraging you to keep pushing forward.

Positive reinforcement is more than just a psychological concept; it's a practical tool for self-improvement. When you reward yourself for achieving a goal, your brain releases dopamine, a chemical that makes you feel good. This positive feedback loop boosts your self-esteem and motivates you to continue the behaviors that led to success. It's like giving your brain a high-five for a job well done. Over time, this process can transform your mindset, making challenges feel less daunting and more like opportunities to prove what you can do. By consistently acknowledging and rewarding your progress, you tell yourself that your efforts matter and are worth celebrating.

Adopting a continual growth mindset means viewing each success as a stepping stone to more significant achievements. It's about understanding that every small win is part of a more extensive journey toward personal development. This mindset encourages you to keep learning and improving, no matter how much you've achieved. It's like being a gardener, nurturing each plant with care, knowing it will blossom one day. Encouraging this mindset in teens is crucial. It helps them see that the path to success isn't a straight line but a series of small steps, each building on the last. By focusing on growth rather than perfection, they learn to appreciate the process as much as the outcome.

Interactive Element: Daily Success Tracker

Create a simple chart with columns for the date, the task or goal completed, and a space for reflection on how it felt to achieve it. Please take a moment to complete it daily, acknowledging even the most minor accomplishments. Reflect on how these successes contribute to your larger goals and consider sharing them with friends or family to build a supportive community around your growth.

Recognizing progress and celebrating achievements isn't just about feeling good at the moment. It's about building a solid foundation for future success. Each small win is a building block, contributing to the larger structure of your dreams and aspirations. As you continue to acknowledge and celebrate these steps, you foster a sense of confidence and motivation that propels you forward, ready to tackle whatever comes next.

Learning from Failure: Embracing Mistakes

Have you ever felt the sting of failure, like when you didn't make the team or bombed a test you prepared for? It's easy to think of failure as a dead end, but what if we saw it differently? What if failure was simply feedback—a way to learn and grow? This perspective shift can turn setbacks into powerful opportunities for personal growth and resilience. By analyzing what went wrong, you can identify areas for improvement. Maybe you didn't prepare as thoroughly as you thought or need to change your approach. This analysis isn't about dwelling on mistakes; it's about extracting valuable lessons to guide you toward success.

Consider Thomas Edison, who famously failed thousands of times before successfully inventing the lightbulb. Each attempt taught him something new, a critical knowledge that eventually led to his triumph.

Edison's story is a testament to perseverance and the power of learning from failure. Similarly, J.K. Rowling faced numerous rejections before a publisher took a chance on "Harry Potter." Her journey to success was paved with setbacks, yet she persisted, believing in her story's potential. These examples remind us that failure isn't a reflection of our worth but a stepping stone to achieving greatness. They show that even the most successful individuals encounter obstacles, but their response to those challenges sets them apart.

Processing and learning from mistakes involves a methodical approach. Begin with a post-failure analysis. Reflect on what happened, considering every angle. Ask yourself: What went wrong? What could I have done differently? This reflection isn't about self-blame but understanding the situation more clearly. It's like reviewing a game tape to see where you can improve for next time. Once you've identified the missteps, consider how to apply these insights moving forward. Maybe it's adjusting your study habits, seeking feedback from others, or trying a new strategy altogether. The goal is to use failure as a catalyst for growth, transforming it into a learning experience that enriches your skills and knowledge.

Encouraging a growth mindset is vital in this process. A growth mindset is the belief that abilities and intelligence can develop through dedication and hard work. It's about seeing challenges as learning opportunities, not threats to avoid. Embrace the idea that the brain is like a muscle—it strengthens with use. When you approach failure with this mindset, you view it not as a setback but as an integral part of the learning process. It's a chance to stretch your capabilities and discover new ways to overcome obstacles. This perspective fosters resilience, empowering you to face difficulties with confidence and determination.

As you navigate life's challenges, remember that failure is not the end. It's a natural part of the journey toward achieving your goals. By redefining failure as a learning opportunity, you unlock the potential for growth and transformation. Each misstep becomes a stepping stone, guiding you toward more tremendous success and fulfillment. Embrace your mistakes, learn from them, and let them propel you on your path to personal and academic achievement.

Support Systems: Leaning on Your Squad

Imagine standing on a stage, about to give a speech. Your heart is racing, and your palms are sweaty, but you see your best friend and family cheering you on in the front row. That support makes all the difference. A strong support network can be a lifeline, offering the emotional backing you need to face life's challenges. Friends, family, and mentors provide more than just a shoulder to cry on; they are the pillars that help you stand firm when everything else feels shaky. Close friends offer emotional support, listen to your troubles, and celebrate your successes. They're the ones who know when you need a pep talk or just a quiet moment together. With their unconditional love, the family provides a sense of belonging and security. They are like the roots of a tree, grounding you even when the winds of change blow hard. Mentors, whether teachers, coaches, or older siblings, offer guidance and wisdom. They share their experiences, helping you navigate life's complexities more clearly. These relationships are crucial for building resilience and confidence, reminding you that you're not alone in your struggles.

Building and maintaining these support networks requires effort and intention. It's about creating meaningful relationships that enrich your life, not just collecting acquaintances. Start by engaging with community groups or clubs that align with your interests. Whether it's a sports team, a drama club, or a volunteer group, these communities offer a space to connect with like-minded individuals and form lasting bonds. Reach out to people who inspire you, and don't hesitate to ask for advice or mentorship. It's okay to seek help; it's a sign of strength, not weakness. By asking for guidance, you learn from others and show them that you value their insight. Maintaining these relationships means being present and available and offering support in return. It's a two-way street where giving is just as important as receiving.

Reciprocal support strengthens these bonds, enhancing resilience. When you support others, you create a network of care that uplifts everyone involved. Imagine a group project where each member plays to their strengths, helping each other succeed. The collective effort not only achieves the goal but also builds a sense of camaraderie and trust. This reciprocity fosters an environment where everyone feels valued and empowered, knowing they have a reliable network to lean on. It's like weaving a safety net; each thread represents a relationship that holds you up when you falter.

Encouraging teens to reach out for support is crucial. It's common to feel hesitant, fearing judgment or rejection. But seeking help is a courageous act that opens doors to growth and understanding. It's about recognizing that everyone needs a little help sometimes and that asking for it doesn't make you weak; it makes you human. Start by sharing your challenges with a trusted friend or family member. They might have faced similar issues and can offer valuable advice. Building a support network takes time, but the benefits are lasting. It's about creating a circle of trust where you can be yourself fully and authentically.

As we wrap up this chapter, remember that support systems aren't just beneficial; they're vital. They provide the foundation for resilience, confidence, and growth. With a strong network, you can face challenges with courage and assurance. Next, we'll explore how to navigate social pressures, equipping you with tools to maintain your well-being in a connected world.

Chapter 7: Engaging Parents and Guardians

Keep Growing, Stay Grounded, and Own Your Story

Imagine standing on a bridge over a wide river, the water rushing below and the banks stretching apart on either side. The bridge symbolizes the connection between generations, linking the experiences and values of parents and teens. Yet, sometimes, the bridge feels shaky, swaying with misunderstandings and miscommunication. This generational gap space is filled with different perspectives shaped by unique historical, social, and technological contexts. As teens, you might find it easy to text or post a quick story while your parents remember when face-to-face conversations were the norm. This digital divide can create tension, as parents may struggle to keep up with the rapid pace of technological change, leading to friction in communication styles. Recognizing these differences is the first step in building a stronger connection, like reinforcing the bridge to withstand the currents below.

For many parents, raising teens today presents challenges that previous generations might not have faced. Technology plays a massive role, not just in communication but in parenting itself. The constant connectivity of smartphones and social media can be overwhelming for parents who grew up without such instant access. Imagine the anxiety of trying to understand a world where likes, comments and online interactions carry as much weight as face-to-face conversations. Economic pressures compound these challenges as parents juggle work, finances, and family responsibilities. These pressures can influence family decisions, from budgeting for necessities to planning vacations. Understanding these struggles can foster empathy, helping teens appreciate the complexities parents navigate daily. It's about seeing beyond the surface and recognizing that behind every decision lies a web of considerations and constraints.

Open conversations about differing viewpoints can transform misunderstandings into opportunities for growth. It's like opening a window in a stuffy room, letting in fresh air and perspectives. One effective strategy is using family dialogue prompts—questions or topics that encourage sharing and listening. These prompts can be simple yet powerful, like asking, "What's something you wish I understood better about your world?" or "How can we better support each other?" Such questions invite honesty and reflection, creating a space where both teens and parents feel heard and valued. These conversations aren't about winning an argument but exploring each other's realities with curiosity and respect. It's like weaving threads into a tapestry, where each story adds richness and depth.

Appreciating parental wisdom can be a game-changer in approaching life's challenges. Parents bring a wealth of experience, often learned through trial and error, that can guide you in making informed decisions. Imagine having a map with routes marked by someone who's walked the path before you. By valuing their advice, you tap into this reservoir of knowledge, avoiding pitfalls and embracing opportunities. It's about recognizing that while the world has changed, certain truths remain timeless—like the importance of integrity, kindness, and resilience. These conversations can enhance personal growth as you learn to integrate your parents' insights with your vision of the future.

Interactive Element: Generational Perspective Exercise

Set aside time for a conversation with your parents using the guide below. It starts off with "Share a challenge you faced as a teen and how you overcame it." Listen actively and then share a similar challenge from your own life. Reflect on the similarities and differences and consider how their experience might inform your approach.

Understanding and bridging the generational gap requires patience, empathy, and dialogue. It's about building a partnership where both sides learn from each other, strengthening the bonds that hold families together. This chapter invites you to walk that bridge and engage with the unique perspectives that shape your family's story.

Conversation Guide: Bridging the Generational Gap

This guide will help you engage in a meaningful dialogue with your parents, fostering connection, understanding, and empathy. Use this framework to explore challenges, share stories, and reflect on your shared experiences.

Step 1: Prepare for the Conversation

1. **Set the Stage:**

   o Choose a quiet, comfortable time and place to talk without distractions.

   o Let your parent(s) know you'd like to have a reflective conversation.

   Forexample: *"I'd love to hear about your experiences as a teen and share some of mine. Could we talk sometime soon?"*

2. **Be Open and Curious:**

   o Approach the conversation with a genuine interest in learning from their experiences.

   o Remind yourself to listen without judgment and reflect before responding.

Step 2: Start the Conversation

Use this prompt to begin:

- **Prompt:** *"Can you share a challenge you faced as a teenager and how you overcame it?"*

Step 3: Actively Listen

While they share their story:

1. Practice Active Listening:

- o   Make eye contact, nod, and show you're engaged.
- o   Avoid interrupting or jumping in with your own experiences right away.

2. Ask Open-Ended Questions:

- o   "How did that experience make you feel?"
- o   "What was the biggest lesson you learned from that challenge?"
- o   "Did you have anyone supporting you through it?"

Step 4: Share Your Experience

Once they've finished, respond with gratitude:

o "Thank you for sharing that with me. It's really inspiring to hear how you overcame that."

o Then, share your own story:

o "I faced a similar challenge when I was younger. Here's what happened…"

o Include:

o The context of your challenge.

o How did you feel at the time?

o The steps you took to overcome it (or what you're still working on).

Step 5: Reflect Together

o Explore the similarities and differences in your experiences:

o "It's interesting how we both dealt with [insert similarity]."

o "I hadn't thought about [their approach] before—it gives me a new perspective."

o "Our situations were different in [insert difference], but I can see how your approach might work for me."

Step 6: End on a Positive Note

o   Thank them again: "I really appreciate you sharing that—it helps me see things in a new light."

o   Express what you've learned: "This conversation reminded me of how resilient we both are, and it's given me some great ideas for tackling challenges in the future."

Step 7: Reflect on the Conversation

Take time after the discussion to journal or think about:

•   What insights did I gain from their story?

_____

_____

•   How does their experience inform my own challenges?

_____

_____

•   What surprised me about their perspective or approach?

_____

_____

_____

Tips for Success

o **Be Patient:** Allow the conversation to unfold naturally. Don't rush or pressure them to share.

o **Stay Empathetic:** Remember that their challenges were shaped by a different time and context.

o **Celebrate the Connection:** Acknowledge the value of learning from one another and strengthening your bond.

Family Meetings: Creating a Safe Space for Dialogue

Imagine the living room as a stage, where the whole family gathers regularly, not for a performance, but for genuine conversation. Family meetings are like setting up a consistent date with your loved ones—when everyone can share thoughts, discuss concerns, and celebrate successes. Establishing a regular schedule for these meetings is key. It's like marking a recurring event on the calendar, making sure everyone knows when to show up and what to expect. The sense of routine helps create a comfortable atmosphere where dialogue flows naturally over time. These meetings become a safe harbor in the week's storm, a place to anchor conversations and strengthen connections.

Conducting effective family meetings requires structure but not rigidity. Start by creating an agenda, a simple list of topics to guide the discussion. This isn't about strict adherence but rather about giving the conversation a clear direction. Think of it like a road map; it helps you navigate the meeting without getting lost in tangents. Setting ground rules is equally important, ensuring everyone knows the norms—like taking turns to speak or listening without interruptions. Rotating roles for meeting facilitation can also be beneficial. Allow each family member to lead a meeting, take notes, or keep time. This rotation keeps the process dynamic and empowers everyone to contribute equally. A shared agenda encourages collaboration, making it a collective effort rather than a top-down lecture.

Creating an inclusive environment is vital. Everyone should feel comfortable expressing their thoughts without fear of judgment or dismissal. It fosters a sense of safety where all voices are valued and respected. Imagine the meeting as a circle, where each person's perspective adds a piece to the whole picture. This non-judgmental space encourages openness and honesty, allowing for deeper understanding and connection. It's not just about hearing words but about truly listening and understanding the emotions and intentions behind  them. This atmosphere of acceptance is like fertile soil, nurturing ideas and solutions that might not emerge elsewhere.

Family meetings can cover many topics, from the mundane to the meaningful. Discussing upcoming family outings or activities is a great way to start. Planning a weekend hike or a movie night can spark excitement and collaboration. It's an opportunity to share interests, discover new activities, and create shared experiences. These planning moments can lead to cherished memories, strengthening the bonds that unite everyone. Addressing concerns, like household chores or school challenges, can also be constructive. It's about finding solutions collectively, where everyone's input is considered and valued. These discussions can transform potential conflicts into opportunities for growth and understanding, like turning rough stones into smooth pebbles.

Regular family meetings are more than just a scheduled chat; they are an investment in relationships. They provide a platform for everyone to express themselves, fostering a culture of communication and mutual respect. Over time, these meetings can become a cherished tradition, a cornerstone of family dynamics that supports emotional well-being and unity. Whether planning the next family vacation or discussing a recent disagreement, these meetings offer a space where everyone can be heard, understood, and appreciated.

Negotiation Skills: Finding Middle Ground

Imagine a bustling kitchen on a Saturday morning: everyone's clattering about, bumping into each other, and arguing over who's supposed to clean up and who's making breakfast. It's a familiar scene in many households, where balancing responsibilities can feel like a tug-of-war. Negotiation skills are the key to turning these chaotic moments into smooth operations. In family dynamics, negotiation is not just for resolving conflicts; it's about meeting the needs of everyone involved and creating a harmonious environment where each member feels heard and valued. Consider household responsibilities, for instance. Negotiating who does what can transform a dreaded chore into a shared task. It's like turning a solo performance into a duet, where each person plays their part for a collective win.

Negotiation begins with active listening and empathy, often overlooked but compelling skills. When you truly listen, putting aside your agenda, you open the door to understanding another's perspective. It's about hearing not just the words but the emotions behind them. Empathy allows you to step into someone else's shoes, feel their feelings, and respond with genuine understanding. These skills are the foundation of any successful negotiation, turning potential conflicts into opportunities for connection. Identifying shared interests is another crucial step. It's about finding that sweet spot where everyone's needs overlap and creating a solution that benefits all parties involved. Think of it as finding a shared goal, like planning a family movie night where everyone can choose a film on rotation. It's not about winning or losing but creating a scenario where everyone walks away satisfied.

Flexibility is a vital component of effective negotiation. It's the willingness to bend without breaking, to adapt as the conversation unfolds. Parents and teens can benefit from remaining open-minded and ready to explore alternative solutions if the initial plan doesn't work. This flexibility requires a mindset shift, moving from rigid positions to a space where creativity and compromise thrive. Imagine negotiating the destination for a family vacation. Instead of insisting on a single location, explore multiple options, each offering something for everyone. This approach reduces tension and enriches the experience, allowing for unexpected discoveries and shared memories.

To practice these negotiation skills, try role-playing different family scenarios. Create a situation, like deciding on the family vacation destination, and take turns negotiating each person's preferences. This exercise provides a safe space to experiment with different strategies and test out what works and doesn't. It's a bit like a rehearsal, where you can refine your skills without the pressure of real-world consequences. Through these practice sessions, everyone learns to articulate their needs clearly, listen actively, and find solutions that respect everyone's viewpoints. These skills, once honed, become invaluable tools in navigating the complexities of family life. They transform everyday interactions, making them more collaborative, respectful, and fulfilling.

Negotiation is a lifelong skill that extends beyond the family dynamic into friendships, work, and community interactions. It fosters a culture of mutual respect and understanding, where each voice is valued and each needs to be considered. By mastering negotiation, families can create a home environment that thrives on cooperation and harmony. Potential conflicts are turned into opportunities for growth and connection, laying the foundation for stronger relationships and a more peaceful home life.

Joint Activities: Building Bonds Through Shared Experiences

Picture this: the kitchen is filled with the rich aroma of spices and the sizzling sound of onions hitting the pan. You and your family are gathered around the counter, each person adding their touch to a beloved family recipe. Cooking meals together is more than just an exercise in culinary skills—it's a way to weave memories into the fabric of everyday life. As you mix, chop, and stir, stories flow as freely as the laughter that fills the room. These shared moments in the kitchen become a canvas for connection, where each ingredient is a brushstroke that paints a picture of togetherness. Preparing a meal becomes a ritual that strengthens family bonds, creating a sense of unity and accomplishment everyone can savor, both in taste and spirit.

Beyond the kitchen, the world offers various activities catering to diverse interests and abilities. Imagine the family lacing up their hiking boots, ready to explore a nearby trail. Nature walks are a perfect opportunity to disconnect from the digital world and reconnect with each other. As you wander through the woods, conversations flow naturally, inspired by the beauty of the surroundings. It's a chance to share observations, marvel at the wonders of nature, and enjoy the simple pleasure of each other's company. For those who prefer the comfort of home, a family game night can be just as enriching. Gather around the table for a game of cards or a challenging puzzle, where the competition is friendly, and the laughter is contagious. These activities cater to different skill levels, ensuring everyone can participate and enjoy, regardless of age or ability.

Regular quality time is the glue that holds family relationships together. It's like watering a garden; the more you nurture it, the more it blooms. Consistent participation in shared activities fosters a deeper understanding and empathy, allowing family members to see each other in new and meaningful ways. These moments offer a break from the routine, a pause to appreciate the people who mean the most to you. They remind you that even in the hustle and bustle of daily life, there's always time to connect, listen, and love. It's these shared experiences that create a tapestry of memories woven with threads of laughter, joy, and sometimes even a little chaos.

Creativity is the key to keeping these activities fresh and exciting. Families are encouraged to think outside the box and explore new experiences and traditions that reflect their unique interests and values. This could be as simple as starting a family scrapbook, where each member contributes photos, drawings, or writings about their adventures together. The scrapbook becomes a living document, a testament to shared experiences and memories. The project invites everyone to contribute, fostering a sense of ownership and pride in the family's story. The possibilities are endless, whether trying a new sport, visiting a local museum, or even embarking on a DIY home project. Each new activity is an opportunity to learn, grow, and discover something new about each other, strengthening the bonds that make your family a cherished part of your life.

Encouraging Independence: Trusting Your Teen

Imagine a bird learning to fly. At first, it hesitates, unsure if its wings will hold. It takes a few cautious flaps, then soars with confidence. This is much like the process of encouraging independence in teens. As a parent, the instinct to protect is strong, yet allowing your teen the freedom to make decisions is crucial. It's about finding that spot between guidance and autonomy, where teens learn from their choices but with a safety net below. Gradually increasing responsibilities is one way to support this growth. Start small, perhaps by managing chores or planning their schedule. As they show responsibility, they introduce more complex tasks, like handling personal finances. This progression builds competence and self-assurance, like adding weights to a barbell to build muscle.

The benefits of fostering independence extend far beyond adolescence. Each decision made and responsibility handled prepares teens for the complexities of adulthood. Consider personal finances as a prime example. Teaching teens to budget, save, and even manage a small bank account can instill lifelong skills. It's not just about managing money; it's about understanding the value of resources and making informed choices. When teens learn to rely on themselves, their confidence grows. They begin to see themselves as capable individuals, ready to tackle the world's challenges. This self-reliance is empowering, providing a foundation of confidence supporting all life areas.

Building trust is a two-way street. It starts with consistent communication and mutual respect. Open discussions about expectations are key to fostering this trust. Sit down with your teen and discuss what you both hope to achieve. Discuss boundaries and responsibilities clearly, ensuring everyone is on the same page. This transparency removes ambiguity and sets a framework for accountability. Please share your thoughts, but also listen to theirs. It's about creating a dialogue, not a monologue. When teens feel heard, their willingness to trust and be trusted increases. This mutual respect strengthens the parent-child relationship, creating a partnership where both sides feel valued.

Parents often find themselves balancing the roles of mentor and controller. However, acting as a mentor rather than a controller can significantly enhance a teen's growth. Mentors guide, advise, and support without dictating every move. They empower teens to take ownership of their choices, encouraging them to learn from successes and failures. This approach fosters independence while providing a safety net. Imagine a coach on the sidelines, offering advice and encouragement but ultimately allowing the player to make decisions on the field. This empowers teens to navigate their path, knowing they have someone to turn to for guidance. By acting as mentors, parents help teens develop critical thinking skills and resilience, preparing them for the diverse challenges of adulthood. It's about stepping back just enough to let them soar, knowing you're always there if they need a steady hand.

Professional Help: When to Seek Counseling

Imagine feeling trapped in a room where the walls seem to be closing in, with no apparent way out. This is what persistent mood changes or academic decline feel like for some teens. It's more than just having a bad day or struggling with a tricky subject at school. When these feelings persist over time, they might be signs that professional intervention could be beneficial. You might notice your teen withdrawing from activities they once loved or their grades slipping despite their efforts. These behaviors can signal underlying emotional challenges that need more than a parent's loving support.

Seeking professional help through counseling provides a framework for teens and families to navigate these challenges. Counseling is not about fixing someone but equipping them with tools to understand better and manage their emotions. It's like learning a new language—one that helps articulate feelings, identify triggers, and develop coping strategies. Through therapy, teens can explore their emotions in a safe space, guided by someone trained to listen without judgment. For families, counseling offers insights into dynamics that might contribute to stress, helping everyone learn to communicate more effectively and support each other more fully. It's a proactive step towards building emotional resilience, like strengthening muscles to prevent injury.

Approaching the counseling topic can be sensitive, especially if your teen already feels vulnerable. It's essential to frame counseling as a positive, proactive choice rather than a sign of failure. Start by openly conversing, expressing concern and care rather than blame. You might say, "I've noticed you've been feeling down lately, and I want to ensure you have all the support you need." Emphasize that seeking help is a strength, not a weakness, and that it's okay to reach out when things feel overwhelming. Encourage them to ask questions and express any reservations they might have. This approach fosters a sense of partnership, showing that you're in it together, ready to support them every step of the way.

Choosing the right counselor is crucial for ensuring a positive experience. It's not just about finding someone with the proper credentials but someone who aligns with your family's values and your teen's needs. Start by considering what type of counseling might be most beneficial—individual therapy, family therapy, or perhaps group sessions. Research different professionals, considering factors like their specialization, approach, and availability. Some teens might feel more comfortable with a counselor of a particular gender or age, so consider these preferences. It can also be helpful to schedule a meeting with potential counselors to see how your teen feels in their presence. This initial meeting is like a test drive, allowing one to gauge comfort levels and establish rapport. The goal is to find someone who makes your teen feel understood and supported, creating an environment where they feel safe to explore their emotions.

Counseling can be a pivotal step in a teen's journey toward emotional well-being. It offers a path to understanding and growth, where challenges become opportunities for learning and resilience. By recognizing when professional help is needed, framing it positively, and carefully selecting the right counselor, families can ensure their teens receive the support they need to thrive.

Red Flags Indicating a Teen May Need Help or Counseling

1. **Drastic Changes in Behavior**

   o Sudden withdrawal from family, friends, or activities they once enjoyed.

   o Acting out in ways out of character, such as aggression or defiance.

2. **Significant Academic Decline**

   o Poor performance in school despite previous success.

o   Skipping classes or losing interest in education altogether.

3. **Mood Swings or Emotional Instability**

o   Persistent sadness, anxiety, or irritability.

o   Unexplained outbursts or difficulty managing emotions.

Social Isolation

o   Avoiding social interactions or spending excessive time alone.

o   Struggling to maintain friendships or connect with peers.

4. **Changes in Sleep Patterns**

o   Sleeping too much, struggling with insomnia, or experiencing frequent nightmares

o   Complaints of constant fatigue or low energy.

5. **Appetite or Weight Changes**

o   Noticeable weight loss or gain.

o   Skipping meals, overeating, or developing unhealthy eating habits.

6. **Risky or Self-Destructive Behavior**

   o Experimenting with drugs, alcohol, or unsafe sexual activity.

   o Engaging in dangerous activities without regard for consequences.

7. **Physical Signs of Self-Harm**

   o Unexplained cuts, burns, or bruises.

   o Wear long sleeves or clothing to cover up injuries, even in warm weather.

8. **Expressions of Hopelessness or Low Self-Esteem**

   o Frequent statements like "I'm a failure," "I don't belong," or "What's the point?"

   o A sense of worthlessness or feelings of being unloved.

9. **Talk of Death or Suicidal Thoughts**

   o Talking or joking about death or suicide.

   o Searching online for ways to harm themselves.

Next Steps

If you observe any of these red flags:

- **Approach with Compassion:** Have a nonjudgmental conversation about what they're experiencing.

- **Seek Professional Support:** Contact a school counselor, therapist, or trusted professional for guidance.

- **Stay Involved:** Regularly check in, listen, and offer ongoing support.

Chapter 8: Sustaining Emotional Growth

Sustaining Emotional Growth – Nurturing the Skills for Lifelong Success

Imagine standing in a garden that's been meticulously tended over the years. Every plant and flower reflects the care and effort put into nurturing it. Your emotional growth is much like that garden—it requires regular attention and dedication to flourish. Emotional growth is not a one-time event but a continuous journey, demanding commitment just like tending to a garden does. It's easy to assume your work is done once you've learned a few techniques. However, emotions are dynamic and ever-changing, much like the seasons. They require you to adapt and learn constantly. This ongoing process ensures that your emotional skills remain sharp and ready to tackle whatever life throws your way.

Engaging in workshops and seminars on emotional intelligence can be incredibly beneficial. These sessions provide a space to learn from experts and fellow participants, gaining insights into how others manage their emotions. They offer a chance to practice new skills in a supportive environment, like a rehearsal before a big performance. Consider attending events focusing on emotional intelligence to immerse yourself in the latest research and strategies. They can provide knowledge and practical exercises to incorporate into daily life, helping you better understand and manage your emotions.

Beyond workshops, there are numerous resources available for ongoing self-education. The vast world of books, podcasts, and online courses offers countless opportunities to deepen your emotional skills. Books like "Emotional Intelligence" by Daniel Goleman provide foundational knowledge, while podcasts such as "The Happiness Lab" offer regular insights into emotional well-being. Online courses from Coursera or edX can also provide structured learning, allowing you to explore topics ranging from mindfulness to communication skills. These resources are tools in a toolbox, each offering unique strategies to help you navigate your emotional landscape. Dive into these materials with curiosity and an open mind, and you'll find that there's always something new to learn.

Curiosity plays a crucial role in emotional growth. It's the spark that drives you to explore new ideas and approaches. Imagine approaching your emotions with the same wonder and openness as a child discovering the world. This mindset encourages you to experiment, question, and reflect, leading to deeper self-awareness and understanding. Curiosity allows you to see mistakes not as failures but as opportunities for growth. It invites you to ask questions like, "Why did I react that way?" or "What can I learn from this experience?" By staying curious, you keep your emotional skills sharp and ready for whatever challenges come your way.

Developing a personal growth plan can provide structure and direction for your emotional education. Start by setting clear, achievable goals that align with your values and interests. These goals could be as simple as practicing mindfulness for five minutes each day or as ambitious as completing a course on emotional intelligence. Outline the steps needed to achieve each goal and consider scheduling regular check-ins to track your progress. This plan serves as a roadmap, guiding you toward emotional maturity. A structured approach ensures that you remain focused and motivated, helping you build resilience and confidence.

Interactive Element: Personal Growth Plan Template

The personal growth plan below will help you list three emotional skills you want to improve. Write down specific actions you'll take to develop each skill, such as attending a workshop, reading a book, or practicing a new technique. Set a timeline for achieving these goals and include regular check-ins to assess your progress. This template will serve as a guide, helping you stay on track and measure your growth.

Emotional growth is a lifelong pursuit. You ensure your emotional skills remain vibrant and compelling by continuously learning, exploring new resources, nurturing curiosity, and creating a personal growth plan. This ongoing commitment to self-improvement enhances your emotional intelligence and enriches your relationships and overall well-being.

Personal Growth Plan: Enhancing Emotional Skills

Use this template to identify and develop three emotional skills. Follow the steps below to create actionable goals, set a timeline, and track progress.

1. Emotional Skill #1: (Example: Managing Stress and Anxiety)

- **Specific Actions:**

  1. Practice mindfulness or meditation for 10 minutes daily.

  2. Read a book on stress management (*e.g., "The Anxiety Solution"* by Chloe Brotheridge).

  3. Attend a local or online stress management workshop.

- **Timeline:**

  1. Begin mindfulness practice today.

  2. Complete the book within 4 weeks.

  3. Attend a workshop within 2 months.

- **Check-In Points:**

  1. Weekly: Journal on how mindfulness has impacted your stress levels
     .
  2. Monthly: Reflect on how techniques from the book/ workshop have improved your coping strategies.

---

2. Emotional Skill #2: (Example: Improving Communication Skills)

- **Specific Actions:**

  1. Take an online course on effective communication (*e.g., via Coursera or Udemy*).

  2. Practice active listening by summarizing what others say before responding.

3. Engage in weekly conversations with a trusted friend or mentor to apply new skills.

- **Timeline:**

1. Enroll in an online course within 1 week.

2. Begin practicing active listening daily.

3. Schedule weekly conversations starting this week.

- **Check-In Points:**

1. Weekly: Reflect on how communication techniques are applied in real-life conversations.

2. End of course: Assess your growth and areas needing more attention.

---

3. Emotional Skill #3: (Example: Cultivating Gratitude and Positivity)

- **Specific Actions:**

1. Write down three things you're grateful for every evening.

2. Read a book on gratitude (*e.g.,* *"The Gratitude Diaries"* by Janice Kaplan).

3. Volunteer or perform small acts of kindness weekly to foster a sense of contribution.

- **Timeline:**

1. Begin gratitude journaling today.

2. Finish the book within 6 weeks.

3. Commit to weekly acts of kindness starting this weekend.

- **Check-In Points:**

    1. Weekly: Reflect on how gratitude journaling and acts of kindness have influenced your mood.

    2. Monthly: Assess how gratitude has shifted your outlook and   mindset.

Tracking and Reflection

1. Use this space to log your progress for each emotional skill:

Skill 1 Progress:

Skill 2 Progress:

Skill 3 Progress:

- **Questions for Reflection:**

  o What successes am I seeing in my personal growth?

  _____

  o What challenges am I facing, and how can I overcome them?

  _____

  o How have these changes impacted my emotional well-being and relationships?

  _____

  _____

Conclusion By continuously learning, exploring new resources, and nurturing curiosity, you ensure your emotional skills remain vibrant and compelling. Use this journal as a living document to guide and measure your personal growth. Commit to self-improvement, and watch as it enriches your relationships, emotional intelligence, and overall life satisfaction.

Reflective Practices: Regular Check-Ins with Yourself

Imagine standing before a mirror, not just seeing your reflection but truly looking within. Regular self-reflection is like holding that mirror up to your emotions and actions, allowing you to track your progress and pinpoint areas for growth. It's a valuable practice that can reveal patterns in your behavior, helping you understand why you react the way you do. Think of it as a personal check-in, a dedicated time to pause and ask yourself, "How am I doing?" This kind of introspection is more than just thinking about your day. It's about digging deeper, exploring your emotional responses, and identifying what might hold you back or propel you forward.

One way to engage in effective self-reflection is through weekly self-assessment exercises. Set aside time weekly to sit with your thoughts and evaluate your emotional journey. Ask yourself questions like, "What went well this week?" or "What challenges did I face, and how did I handle them?" This practice isn't about criticizing yourself but rather understanding your emotional landscape. It's like reviewing a map before setting out on a road trip, ensuring you know where you've been and where you're headed. By consistently engaging in these exercises, you gain a clearer picture of your emotional health and can adjust as needed.

Techniques such as journaling, meditation, or self-questioning can facilitate this introspection. Journaling lets you capture your thoughts and feelings on paper, providing a tangible record of your emotional experiences. Use reflective journaling prompts to guide your writing. For instance, consider prompts like "Describe a moment this week when you felt most at peace" or "What triggered strong emotions, and how did you manage them?" These questions encourage you to explore your inner world and gain insights into your behavior. Meditation offers another path to reflection, where you focus inward, observing your thoughts without judgment. It's a chance to quiet the noise and listen to your inner voice. Self-questioning, too, can be a powerful tool. It involves asking yourself targeted questions, like, "What am I grateful for today?" or "What could I have done differently in that situation?"

Integrating these practices into your daily or weekly routine ensures consistent reflection. It might be a few minutes before bed each night or a more extended session on a Sunday afternoon. The key is to make it a regular habit, something you look forward to as a time for personal growth. Consider blocking this time off your calendar, treating it as an essential appointment with yourself. This dedicated space allows you to step back from the busyness of life and focus on what truly matters—your emotional well-being.

Tracking emotional changes over time can lead to greater self-awareness and growth. Observing patterns in your responses, you begin to notice what triggers certain emotions and how you typically react. Perhaps you realize that stress at school often leads to irritability at home or that spending time with friends lifts your mood. These observations empower you to make informed choices. You might incorporate stress-relief techniques or prioritize activities that bring you joy. With time, you'll see how small changes in your routine or mindset can significantly improve your emotional health.

Interactive Element: Reflective Journaling Prompts

Use the list of reflective journaling prompts below to guide your introspection. These prompts include questions like, "What was a highlight of my day?" and "What lesson did I learn this week?" Use these prompts as a starting point for journaling sessions, allowing you to delve deeper into your thoughts and emotions.

Embracing reflective practices as part of your life enriches your understanding of yourself. It's not just about looking back but also about looking forward, using the insights gained to shape a more emotionally aware and resilient future.

1. Daily Highlights

- What was the highlight of my day?

_____

_____

_____

- What made me smile or feel grateful today?

_____

_____

_____

_____

2. Emotional Check-In

- How am I feeling right now?

_____

_____

_____

- What emotions did I experience most strongly today, and why?

_____

_____

_____

_____

3. Growth and Lessons

- What lesson did I learn this week?

_____

_____

_____

- How did I step out of my comfort zone recently?

_____

_____

_____

_____

4. Gratitude and Positivity

- What are three things I am grateful for today?

_____

_____

_____

- Who or what made me feel supported this week?

_____

_____

_____

_____

5. Challenges and Problem-Solving

- What challenge did I face today, and how did I overcome it?

_____

_____

_____

- How can I approach this problem differently in the future?

_____

_____

_____

6. Personal Aspirations

- What is one goal I want to focus on this week?

_____

_____

_____

- How am I progressing toward my long-term goals?

_____

_____

_____

7. Self-Care and Balance

- Did I care for myself physically, emotionally, and mentally today?

_____

_____

_____

- What can I do to recharge and nurture myself tomorrow?

_____

_____

_____

_____

8. Relationships and Connections

- Who made me feel valued and loved today?

_____

_____

_____

- Is there a relationship in my life I want to nurture more?

_____

_____

_____

_____

9. Mindfulness and Awareness

- What is something I noticed today that I usually overlook?

_____

_____

_____

- How present was I in my interactions and activities today?

_____

_____

_____

_____

10. Dreams and Creativity

- What have I been dreaming about but haven't pursued yet?

_____

_____

_____

- How can I incorporate more creativity or passion into my life?

_____

_____

_____

Giving Back: Helping Others Manage Their Emotions

Imagine standing at the front of a room, with voices buzzing around you as you prepare to lead a discussion. Your heart quickens, not with fear, but with excitement. You're about to guide your peers through a conversation about managing emotions—a topic you've been exploring deeply. It's a moment where everything you've learned  begins to flow outward, transforming your life and those around you. Supporting others on their emotional journeys is like looking into a mirror: your understanding deepens as you teach and mentor. You reinforce your skills whenever you help someone else manage their feelings. It's an empowering realization that your experiences and insights can impact others, prompting you to grow even more.

Volunteering as a peer counselor or mentor provides a meaningful avenue for this kind of growth. Picture yourself sitting across from a friend, offering a listening ear and gentle guidance. In these moments, your empathy and patience are invaluable. These skills, honed over time, become essential tools in creating a supportive environment where others feel safe to express themselves. As a mentor, you're helping someone else navigate their emotions and learning to navigate your own with more remarkable finesse. Consider getting involved in school or community programs that focus on peer support. These roles offer a chance to build connections, develop leadership skills, and make a tangible difference in the lives of others.

Opportunities for emotional support roles are plentiful. Think about leading a support group or club dedicated to emotional well-being. Imagine the impact of creating a space where teens can come together to share their struggles and triumphs. This kind of leadership requires empathy and active listening, which are crucial for supporting others effectively. When you actively listen, you offer your full attention, creating a sense of validation and understanding. It's about being present and truly hearing what the other person is saying beyond just their words. This approach fosters trust and encourages open communication, laying the foundation for meaningful connections and emotional growth.

Community service projects also provide an excellent platform for promoting emotional well-being. You may volunteer at a local shelter, school, or community center, engaging in uplifting and inspiring activities. Through these projects, you contribute to the community and cultivate a more profound sense of purpose and fulfillment. Think about organizing workshops on stress management or mindfulness, providing practical tools for emotional health. These projects offer a unique chance to connect with individuals from diverse backgrounds, broadening your perspective and enhancing your empathy. As you work alongside others, you realize the power of collective effort in fostering positive change.

In giving back, you discover a profound truth: helping others manage their emotions is reciprocal. Each interaction, every shared experience, becomes a learning opportunity, allowing you to refine your emotional skills. You find yourself more attuned to your feelings and more aware of your strengths and areas for growth. This cycle of support and learning creates a ripple effect, extending beyond individual encounters to impact entire communities. As you continue to engage in these roles, you gain confidence in your ability to make a difference in your life and those around you.

Staying Inspired: Finding Motivation in Others

Imagine the feeling of discovering a story that resonates so profoundly that it lights a fire within you. That's the power of inspiration—it's contagious and transformative. Learning from the stories and achievements of others can be a catalyst for your personal growth. Consider the biographies of emotionally intelligent individuals, where real-life narratives showcase resilience, empathy, and determination. These stories serve as roadmaps, illustrating how others have navigated their paths with grace despite challenges. By absorbing their experiences, you can gain insights into your journey, find motivation in their triumphs, and learn from their setbacks.

Sources of inspiration are all around us, waiting to be discovered. Influential figures such as Malala Yousafzai or Nelson Mandela offer profound lessons in courage and empathy. Books like "Becoming" by Michelle Obama or "The Power of Now" by Eckhart Tolle invite you to explore new perspectives and deepen your understanding of yourself and the world. Podcasts like Brené Brown's "Unlocking Us" or TED Talks on emotional intelligence can ignite a passion for self-improvement. These resources are more than just words; they are seeds of inspiration, ready to grow into meaningful change in your life. By immersing yourself in these stories and ideas, you open yourself to new possibilities and expand your emotional horizons.

Surrounding yourself with positive influences is another way to sustain your growth. Imagine building a network of supportive friends, mentors, and role models who inspire you to be your best self. These individuals become your safety net, offering encouragement and guidance when needed. They help you see your potential, even when you doubt yourself. You create an environment where emotional growth can thrive by spending time with people who uplift and challenge you. This network is not just about receiving support;

it's also about giving back, creating a cycle of inspiration and empowerment that benefits everyone involved.

Finding mentors who exemplify emotional intelligence can provide invaluable guidance. A mentor doesn't have to be a famous figure; they could be a teacher, coach, or family friend. What matters is their ability to guide you with empathy and wisdom. A mentor can offer a fresh perspective on challenges, helping you navigate complex emotions and situations. They are like a lighthouse, providing direction and reassurance as you chart your course. Seeking out mentors is an active process involving reaching out and building relationships based on trust and mutual respect. In doing so, you gain access to a wealth of knowledge and experience, enriching your journey toward greater emotional understanding.

Inspiration fuels sustained growth, driving you to explore new heights and overcome obstacles. By engaging with stories of resilience and surrounding yourself with positive influences, you create an environment where emotional growth can flourish. These connections and lessons remind you that you are not alone in your pursuit of self-improvement. Instead, you are part of a larger community of individuals striving to grow and positively impact the world.

Adapting to Change: Embracing New Challenges

Change is one of life's few constants, impacting us all uniquely. Change can be both unsettling and invigorating, starting with moving to a new city, starting at a different school, or adjusting to a new family dynamic. Imagine the first day at a new school: unfamiliar faces, other classrooms, and a new schedule. It might feel overwhelming, but it's also a fresh start, a blank page waiting to be filled with new experiences and friendships. Adapting to change is a vital part of building emotional resilience. It allows you to navigate life's unpredictable nature with grace and confidence. Embracing change means recognizing it as an opportunity rather than something to fear. It's about acknowledging the discomfort that comes with newness while seeing the potential for growth and learning.

So, how do you embrace change with open arms? One powerful approach is adopting a "growth mindset." This concept, popularized by psychologist Carol Dweck, is about believing that abilities and intelligence can be developed with effort and time. Instead of viewing challenges as insurmountable obstacles, a growth mindset encourages you to see them as chances to improve and learn. It's the difference between thinking, "I can't do this," and "I can't do this yet." Shifting your perspective opens you to possibilities you might not have considered. This mindset doesn't eliminate fear but helps you move through it, knowing that each challenge is a stepping stone to greater understanding and capability.

The emotional benefits of adaptability are vast. When you're open to change, you invite new experiences and insights into your life. It's like broadening your horizon, allowing you to see beyond the immediate and familiar. This openness leads to personal growth, as each new experience teaches you something about yourself and the world. Adaptability also builds resilience, equipping you to easily handle future changes and less stress. Picture yourself as a tree that bends with the wind rather than breaking; each gust makes you stronger and more flexible. By embracing change, you expand your comfort zone and increase your capacity for joy and discovery.

Setting goals that push you beyond your comfort zone is an excellent way to embrace change. These goals should challenge you, sparking both excitement and a little bit of nervousness. It could be joining a new club, trying out for a sports team, or starting a creative project you've always wanted to explore. These goals encourage you to enter the unknown, where actual growth happens. They offer a chance to develop new skills and meet people who inspire and support

you. As you pursue these challenges, you'll find that your confidence grows with each step you take. The more you push your boundaries, the more you realize what you can achieve.

Embracing change is about more than reacting to life's shifts—it's about actively seeking growth and embracing the unknown. By developing a growth mindset, remaining adaptable, and setting ambitious goals, you cultivate an environment where personal and emotional development can flourish. Remember, change is not something to be feared but embraced as a constant companion on your path to self-discovery and resilience.

Crafting Your Narrative: Owning Your Story

Imagine your life is a book for a moment, and you write a new page daily. The story is yours, filled with your values, goals, and experiences. This is your narrative, a powerful tool that shapes how you see yourself and how others see you. Teens often feel like they're living stories written by others—parents, teachers, or peers—but the truth is, you are the author of your own life. Crafting your narrative means taking control of your story and ensuring it reflects who you are. It's about deciding what is important to you and what you want your life to be about. Writing a personal mission statement can help with this process. Think of it as your life's North Star, a guiding principle that keeps you focused on what matters most. It's a statement that captures your core values and aspirations, reminding you of your purpose even when life gets chaotic.

To begin crafting your narrative, consider engaging in activities that encourage self-expression. Storytelling workshops or exercises can be beneficial. These activities create a space to explore your past, reflect on your present, and envision your future. You might start by writing short stories or poems about pivotal moments in your life, those times when you learned something new about yourself or overcame a challenge. Sharing these stories can be empowering and enlightening, helping you identify themes and patterns that resonate with your mission. Creating a vision board or timeline can visually map your goals and achievements, visually representing your journey. These exercises are creative outlets and opportunities to articulate your life story and uncover insights into your identity.

Owning your story means embracing your experiences, both the triumphs and the setbacks. It's about accepting your past and using it as a foundation to build your future. When you take control of your narrative, you empower yourself to lead an authentic life. You begin to see that your story is not just a series of events but a reflection of your choices and values. This realization can be incredibly liberating. It allows you to break free from the expectations and labels others might place on you. You start living on your terms, making decisions that align with your true self. This authenticity leads to greater self-confidence and a deeper connection with others as you attract people who appreciate and support the real you.

Sharing your story with others can have a profound impact. It's a way to connect and inspire, showing everyone has their unique path. When you share your journey with peers, you create a space for understanding and empathy. Others might see parts of themselves in your story, realizing they are not alone in their struggles. This connection can foster a sense of community, where individuals support and uplift one another. It's like weaving a tapestry of shared experiences, each thread adding to the richness of the whole. By opening up about your narrative, you encourage others to do the same, creating a ripple effect of authenticity and empowerment that extends beyond your immediate circle.

As you craft and own your narrative, remember that it's a living document that evolves as you grow and change. Your story is not set in stone but is shaped by the choices you make and the experiences you embrace. By actively participating in this process, you cultivate a sense of ownership over your life, guiding it in your desired direction. This chapter is just the beginning, setting the stage for the next phase of your emotional journey. As you continue to explore and define your narrative, you build a foundation for a life filled with purpose and connection.

Family Games

Here are five engaging family games designed to help teens with anger management while fostering communication, emotional regulation, and positive family bonding:

---

1. Feelings Charades

Objective: Improve emotional awareness and expression.

How to Play:

Write different emotions (e.g., frustration, joy, embarrassment, anger, excitement) on slips of paper.

Players take turns acting out the emotion without speaking while others guess.

After each round, discuss ways to manage or express the emotion healthily.

Benefits: Helps teens recognize emotions, develop empathy, and explore strategies to manage feelings.

---

2. Calm Down Relay

Objective: Practice calming techniques under pressure.

How to Play:

Create stations with calming activities (e.g., deep breathing, squeezing a stress ball, coloring a mandala, or naming five things they see).

Players race to complete the calming tasks at each station.

The focus is on completing the tasks mindfully rather than speed.

Benefits: Introduces teens to calming strategies when feeling angry or stressed.

3. The "What If?" Game

Objective: Encourage problem-solving and perspective-taking.

How to Play:

Pose hypothetical anger-inducing scenarios (e.g., "What if your sibling takes something without asking?").

Each player shares how they might react and brainstorm alternative ways to handle the situation calmly.

Discuss the best strategies as a group.

Benefits: Teaches teens to think before reacting and consider alternative approaches to anger.

4. Emotion Jenga

Objective: Facilitate discussion about emotions and coping techniques.

How to Play:

Write questions or prompts on Jenga blocks (e.g., "What helps you calm down when you're angry?" or "Describe a time you handled anger well.").

Players answer the prompt on the block they pull before adding it to the stack.

Benefits: Promotes self-reflection and emotional expression in a fun, interactive format.

---

5. Gratitude & Growth Board Game

Objective: Shift focus from anger to gratitude and problem-solving.

How to Play:

Create a simple board game with spaces that prompt players to share things they are grateful for or challenges they've overcome.

Include spaces encouraging deep breathing or recounting positive moments from the day.

Benefits: Encourages positive thinking and fosters a supportive family environment.

Conclusion

As our journey together comes to a close, it's essential to reflect on the core purpose of this book: to empower you with practical tools to manage anger and emotions, to enhance your self-awareness, and to build meaningful, lasting relationships. Throughout these pages, I have aimed to provide a compassionate and supportive guide for you, the teens, and your parents and guardians. It's about creating an understanding environment where emotional challenges become pathways to growth, self-awareness, and deeper connections.

We started by diving into the roots of anger in Chapter 1, exploring the science behind emotions and how family dynamics, past experiences, and social pressures can influence how you feel. Understanding these aspects helps you see that emotions are natural and manageable. Then, in Chapter 2, we moved on to recognizing emotional triggers and building self-awareness. Here, you learned about identifying the patterns in your responses, which is the first step toward controlling them. We also introduced mindfulness practices and journaling as tools for gaining clarity and perspective.

Chapter 3 focused on practical strategies to manage anger, such as breathing techniques, physical activity, and creative expression. These are immediate tools when emotions run high. Chapter 4 emphasized the importance of strengthening relationships through active listening, effective communication, and empathy. These skills are vital in turning conflicts into discussions and building trust with those around you.

Chapter 5 focused on navigating the pressures of school and social life, discussing managing academic stress, balancing peer approval with self-approval, and handling bullying. Chapter 6 explored building resilience and confidence, highlighting how positive self-talk and celebrating small wins can boost self-esteem and help you bounce back from setbacks.

For parents, Chapter 7 provided insights on bridging generational gaps and fostering open communication, emphasizing the importance of collaboration and understanding in family dynamics. Finally, Chapter 8 encouraged ongoing emotional growth, reflecting on how embracing change and crafting your narrative can empower you to own your story.

The key takeaways from this journey are simple yet powerful. Emotional intelligence is your ally, helping you navigate life with empathy and understanding. Resilience allows you to turn challenges into growth opportunities, and strong communication skills are the foundation of healthy relationships. These are skills worth nurturing, as they can profoundly impact your life and the lives of those around you.

I encourage you, the teens, to apply what you've learned here. Embrace your emotions and let them guide you to personal growth. Practice the exercises and strategies we've discussed. Don't hesitate to seek support when you need it—whether from friends, family, or professionals. Remember, asking for help is a sign of strength, not weakness.

Your role as parents and guardians is crucial. Continue fostering those open dialogues and supporting your teens' emotional journeys. Your understanding and collaboration can make all the difference in strengthening family bonds and creating a supportive home environment.

This book is just the beginning. I urge you to keep learning and growing. Explore additional resources, participate in community activities, and maintain a mindset open to new experiences and insights. Emotional development is a lifelong journey; there's always more to discover.

Thank you for embarking on this journey with me. Your willingness to learn and grow is inspiring, and I am grateful to have been part of your path toward emotional intelligence and fulfillment. Resources and support are always available, and you are not alone in this journey.

I want to leave you with hope and confidence as we close this chapter. You have the tools to navigate life's challenges and build a future filled with meaningful connections and emotional well-being. Trust yourself and the skills you've gained, and know you can lead a fulfilling and emotionally intelligent life.

References

- *The Neurobiology of the Emotional Adolescent.* Retrieved from *https://pmc.ncbi.nlm.nih.gov/articles/PMC5074886/*

- *Puberty: Tanner Stages for Boys and Girls.* Cleveland Clinic. Retrieved from *https://my.clevelandclinic.org/health/body/puberty#:~:text=Hormones%20involved%20in%20puberty%20include,the%20testes%20to%20produce%20testosterone.*

- *The Role of Family Dynamics in Teen Mental Health.* Retrieved from *https://www.wingswithin.in/article/the-role-of-family-dynamics-in-teen-mental-health*

- *How Using Social Media Affects Teenagers.* Retrieved from *https://childmind.org/article/how-using-social-media-affects-teenagers/*

- *Teaching Emotional Intelligence to Teens and Students.* Retrieved from *https://positivepsychology.com/teaching-emotional-intelligence/*

- *Mindfulness Exercises (for Teens).* Nemours KidsHealth. Retrieved from *https://kidshealth.org/en/teens/mindful-exercises.html*

- *The Mental Health Benefits of Journaling for Teens.* Retrieved from *https://tillyslifecenter.org/2022/10/25/journaling-for-teens-mental-health-resources/*

- *Decoding the Myers-Briggs Type Indicator (MBTI): Evaluating Its Strengths and Limitations.* Retrieved from *https://www.theteenmagazine.com/decoding-the-myers-briggs-type-indicator-mbti-evaluating-its-strengths-and-limitations#:~:text=Teenagers%20are%20in%20a%20constant,strengths%2C%20weaknesses%2C%20and%20motivations.*

- *Breathing Exercises for Stress*. NHS. *Retrieved from* https://www.nhs.uk/mental-health/self-help/guides-tools-and-activities/breathing-exercises-for-stress/

- *Help Your Teen Get More Exercise*. Mayo Clinic Health System. *Retrieved from* https://www.mayoclinichealthsystem.org/hometown-health/speaking-of-health/teens-and-exercise

- *14 Engaging Art Therapy Ideas for Teens to Unlock Healing*. *Retrieved from* https://occasion.app/blog/art-therapy-activities-for-teens

- *Teens and Social Media Use: What's the Impact?* Mayo Clinic. *Retrieved from* https://www.mayoclinic.org/healthy-lifestyle/tween-and-teen-health/in-depth/teens-and-social-media-use/art-20474437

- *How to Practice Active Listening: 16 Examples & Techniques*. *Retrieved from* https://positivepsychology.com/active-listening-techniques/

- *The Root of Teen Empathy Begins with Secure Relationships*. CNN. *Retrieved from* https://www.cnn.com/2021/07/15/health/teen-empathy-secure-family-relationships-wellness/index.html

- *10 Trust-Building Exercises for Kids and Teens*. Healthline. *Retrieved from* https://www.healthline.com/health/parenting/trust-exercises-for-kids

- *Creating Safe Boundaries for Teens to Push Against*. *Retrieved from* https://parentandteen.com/creating-safe-boundaries/

- *13 Practical Time Management Skills to Teach Teens*. *Retrieved from* https://lifeskillsadvocate.com/blog/13-practical-time-management-skills-to-teach-teens/

- *Social Media and Youth Mental Health*. HHS. *Retrieved from* https://www.hhs.gov/surgeongeneral/priorities/youth-mental-health/social-media/index.html

- *How to Resist Peer Pressure & Stand Up for Yourself.* WikiHow. Retrieved from https://www.wikihow.com/Resist-Peer-Pressure

- *Stress Management and Teens.* AACAP. Retrieved from https://www.aacap.org/AACAP/Families_and_Youth/Facts_for_Famili es/FFF-Guide/Helping-Teenagers-With-Stress-066.aspx

- *Resilience: 5 Ways to Help Children and Teens Learn It.* Harvard Health. Retrieved from https://www.health.harvard.edu/blog/resilience-5-ways-to-help-children-and-teens-learn-it-202202242694

- *The Impact of Positive Self-Talk on Teen Confidence and Motivation.* Retrieved from https://teencoachacademy.com/blog/teen-confidence-and-motivation/

- *SMART Goal Setting for Students.* Retrieved from https://www.asvabprogram.com/media-center-article/65

- *8 Famous People Who Overcame Obstacles.* Familius. Retrieved from https://familius.com/8-famous-people-who-overcame-obstacles/?srsltid=AfmBOorPQuCRyev4lWlu_fefrVcbfXw2y8cItQ3TcNk MGtV9dZWhPPU4

- *How Does the Generation Gap Affect Relationships?* Retrieved from https://mindbodycounselingreno.com/blog/relationships/generation-gap/

- *10 Tips for Successful Family Meetings.* Colorado State University Extension. Retrieved from https://extension.colostate.edu/topic-areas/family-home-consumer/10-tips-for-successful-family-meetings/

- *Negotiation with Your Children: How to Resolve Family Conflicts.* Harvard. Retrieved from https://www.pon.harvard.edu/daily/conflict-resolution/negotiating-with-your-children-2/

- ***The Benefits of Family Bonding Activities.*** *Retrieved from* <u>*https://www.pontchartrainpediatrics.com/the-benefits-of-family-bonding-activities*</u>

- ***Peer-to-Peer Mental Health Support.*** *Retrieved from* <u>*https://www.schoolhealthcenters.org/resources/student-impact/peer-support/*</u>

- ***Lucy Hone: 3 Secrets of Resilient People | TED Talk.*** *Retrieved from* <u>*https://www.ted.com/talks/lucy_hone_3_secrets_of_resilient_people?language=en*</u>

Leave a Review!

Thank you for reading *Anger Management for Teens: Mad to Calm*! We'd love to hear your thoughts if you found the strategies helpful, the exercises insightful, or the examples relatable. Your feedback helps us grow and helps others discover tools to manage their emotions and build confidence. Please take a moment to leave a review and share how this book has impacted your journey. Your voice matters!

Website link attach :

Amazon Link Attach:

www.ingramcontent.com/pod-product-compliance
Lightning Source LLC
Chambersburg PA
CBHW071742120626
46550CB00002B/633